SOULFUL PILGRIMAGE

EXPLORING SPIRITUAL JOURNEYS IN INDIA

DR. MINAKSHI BANSAL

DEDICATION

To the seekers, the wanderers, and the curious souls who yearn to explore the depths of their inner being and connect with the divine. May this book inspire you to embark on your own soulful pilgrimage, to discover the hidden treasures that lie within, and to embrace the diversity and richness of India's spiritual traditions.

ᐯᐯᐯ

Contents

Contents

Contents

Prayer

"Om Bhadram Karnebhih Shrinuyama Devah

Bhadram Pashyemakshabhiryajatrah

Sthirairangais Tushtuvamsastanubhih

Vyashema Devahitam Yadayuh

Svasti Na Indro Vriddhashravah

Svasti Nah Pusha Vishwavedah

Svasti Nastarkshyo Arishtanemih

Svasti No Brihaspatir Dadhatu

Om Shantih Shantih Shantih"

This mantra is a prayer for universal well-being, invoking the blessings of various deities for protection, health, and happiness. It emphasizes the importance of experiencing the auspicious through all senses and living a life aligned with divine purpose. The repetition of "Shantih" at the end signifies a deep desire for peace in the individual, the environment, and the universe at large. This mantra is often recited as a prayer for peace, prosperity, and the physical and spiritual well-being of all beings.

ppp

About The Author

This book represents the culmination of extensive research and meticulous analysis, incorporating a diverse range of sources, including numerous books, scholarly studies, and personal experiences. Additionally, I have scoured various websites to gather relevant information and data essential for the compilation of this work. I have taken every precaution to ensure the accuracy of the information presented and have diligently cited all sources to acknowledge their contributions.

From her earliest days, Minakshi was distinguished by an insatiable appetite for reading. Her literary universe was inhabited by characters and narratives that spanned ethical tales, motivational and inspirational stories, and the mythic parables imbued with life lessons. This voracious reading habit was not merely for personal edification but was driven by a desire to distill and disseminate the essence of these narratives to foster the development of students and peers alike. She was particularly captivated by the lives and teachings of historical figures and spiritual leaders such as Adi Shankaracharya, Swami Vivekananda, Dr. APJ Abdul Kalam, Mahamana Pandit Madan Mohan Malviya, Mahatma Gandhi, Sardar Vallabhai Patel, and Vinoba Bhave, among others. Their philosophies and life stories fueled her ambition to embody their ideals of resilience, selflessness, and relentless pursuit of knowledge.

Dr. Minakshi's academic and practical engagement with psychology has been equally noteworthy. As a research scholar, her focus has been on exploring the intricate tapestry of the human psyche, aiming to unlock the potential for psychological well-being and societal harmony. Her scholarly work is complemented by her active involvement in social work, where she employs her academic insights to make tangible differences in the lives of the underprivileged. Her endeavours in social work are characterized by an innovative approach that combines traditional wisdom with contemporary psychological practices to address the multifaceted challenges faced by these communities.

Her artistic talents, another facet of her diverse capabilities, are not merely a personal passion but also serve as a medium through which she communicates and connects with others. Her art, rich in symbolism and emotional depth, reflects her philosophical inquiries and social concerns, offering viewers a glimpse into the breadth of her intellect and the depth of her compassion.

In addition to her contributions to the arts and social sciences, Dr. Minakshi has embraced the healing arts of Pranic Healing, mastering the techniques developed by Master Choa Kok Sui. This practice, which focuses on the manipulation of Prana or life energy to heal the body and aura, has been both a personal journey of discovery and a means through which she extends her healing touch to others. Her proficiency in Pranic Healing is complemented by her advocacy and teaching of various forms of meditation aimed at rejuvenation, personal betterment, and the cultivation of harmony within individuals and communities alike.

Dr. Minakshi's life is a narrative of relentless pursuit, not just of personal achievement but of the upliftment and empowerment of society at large. Her diverse interests and talents—spanning the arts, literature, psychology, and the healing practices—converge on a singular path of service. She embodies the spirit of the luminaries who inspired her, channelling their legacy through her actions and teachings. Through her books, art, and social initiatives, she continues to inspire a new generation to embark on their own journeys of self-discovery, resilience, and altruism.

Her commitment to social betterment, particularly her focus on uplifting underprivileged children, reflects a deep understanding of the transformative potential of education and personal development. By integrating her knowledge of psychology, her artistic sensibilities, and her healing practices, Dr. Bansal has developed a holistic approach to social work that addresses both the immediate needs and the long-term well-being of the communities she serves.

As an author, Dr. Minakshi's writings offer a blend of inspirational insights, practical wisdom, and reflective contemplations drawn from her extensive reading and life experiences. Her books serve as a guide for those seeking to navigate the complexities of life with grace, resilience, and purpose. Through her narratives, she extends an invitation to her readers to explore the depths of their own potential and to contribute meaningfully to the collective well-being of society.

In Dr. Minakshi Bansal, we find a remarkable synthesis of the artist, the scholar, the healer, and the social activist. Her life's work stands as a beacon of hope and a source of inspiration for individuals seeking to make a difference in the world. Her story is a compelling reminder of the power of individual action, rooted in compassion and driven by a profound commitment to the betterment of humanity. Dr. Minakshi's legacy is not just in the tangible outcomes of her efforts but in the enduring spirit of inquiry, empathy, and service that she embodies.

ppp

Preface

In the tapestry of life, there are journeys that transcend the physical realm, journeys that delve deep into the recesses of our souls and ignite a spark of divine connection. India, a land steeped in spirituality and ancient wisdom, has been a beacon for such soulful pilgrimages for centuries. It is a land where the sacred and the mundane intertwine, where temples and ashrams echo with the chants of devotion, and where the pursuit of truth and inner peace finds fertile ground.

The inspiration for this book, "Soulful Pilgrimage: Exploring Spiritual Journeys in India," stemmed from my own profound experiences traversing this land of mystique and enchantment. As a woman seeking a deeper understanding of myself and the world around me, I embarked on a series of pilgrimages across India, each one leading me closer to the elusive truth that lies within.

My journey began in Varanasi, the eternal city on the banks of the sacred Ganges River. Here, amidst the labyrinthine alleyways and the vibrant ghats, I witnessed the cycle of life and death unfold in its raw and unfiltered form. The sights, sounds, and smells of Varanasi overwhelmed my senses, awakening me to the impermanence of existence and the eternal dance of creation and dissolution.

From Varanasi, I ventured to Rishikesh, the yoga capital of the world. Nestled amidst the foothills of the Himalayas, Rishikesh provided a tranquil haven for introspection and spiritual practice. The ashrams and yoga schools that dot the city's landscape offered a plethora of teachings and techniques aimed at cultivating inner peace, mindfulness, and self-awareness. The rhythmic flow of the Ganges, the gentle rustling of leaves, and the melodious chants of mantras created a symphony of serenity that soothed my soul.

My pilgrimage then led me to Haridwar, the gateway to the gods. The Kumbh Mela, a grand religious festival held every twelve years, was in full swing, and I was swept away by the sheer magnitude and fervor of devotion that permeated the atmosphere. Millions of pilgrims from all walks of life had gathered to take a dip in the holy waters of the Ganges, seeking purification and blessings. The experience was both humbling and exhilarating, reminding me of the power of faith and the collective yearning for spiritual connection.

Amritsar, the home of the Golden Temple, was my next destination. The Golden Temple, a beacon of Sikh devotion and a symbol of unity and equality, left me awestruck with its architectural grandeur and spiritual ambiance. The langar, or community kitchen, where thousands of devotees are served free meals every day, was a testament to the Sikh principle of selfless service and the importance of sharing and caring for others.

Bodh Gaya, where Gautama Buddha attained enlightenment, was a place of profound reverence and introspection. The Mahabodhi Temple, a UNESCO World Heritage Site, stands as a majestic testament to the Buddha's teachings of compassion, wisdom, and non-violence. The Bodhi tree, under which the Buddha meditated, is a living symbol of the potential for enlightenment that resides within each of us.

Dharamshala, the abode of the Dalai Lama, offered a glimpse into the vibrant Tibetan culture and spirituality that thrives in exile. The Tsuglagkhang Complex, the Dalai Lama's official residence, is a place of immense significance for Tibetans and Buddhists alike. The complex's temples, monasteries, and libraries are a treasure trove of Tibetan history, culture, and spiritual teachings.

My journey through India continued, taking me to Tirupati, Rameshwaram, Madurai, Kanchipuram, Ujjain, Pushkar, Dwarka,

Mathura, Vrindavan, Ajmer, and Shirdi. Each of these destinations offered a unique spiritual experience, enriching my understanding of India's diverse religious and cultural traditions.

In Tirupati, I witnessed the unwavering devotion of millions of pilgrims who flocked to the Tirumala Venkateswara Temple, seeking the blessings of Lord Venkateswara. In Rameshwaram, I was captivated by the Ramanathaswamy Temple's architectural grandeur and its association with the epic Ramayana. In Madurai, I marveled at the Meenakshi Amman Temple's intricate carvings and sculptures, a testament to the Dravidian art and architecture.

Kanchipuram, with its thousand temples, offered a glimpse into the city's rich religious and cultural heritage. Ujjain, the abode of the Mahakaleshwar Jyotirlinga, drew me into the mystical world of Lord Shiva and his transformative power. Pushkar, with its sacred lake and the Brahma Temple, provided a unique spiritual experience, unlike any other.

Dwarka, believed to be the ancient kingdom of Lord Krishna, transported me to a realm of mythology and legend. The Dwarkadhish Temple, with its towering spires and intricate carvings, is a testament to the city's rich cultural heritage. Mathura and Vrindavan, the birthplace and childhood abode of Lord Krishna, exuded an aura of divine love and devotion.

Ajmer, home to the Dargah Sharif, the revered shrine of the Sufi saint Khwaja Moinuddin Chishti, offered a glimpse into the mystical world of Sufism. The shrine's qawwali music, with its soulful melodies and poetic lyrics, transported me to a state of spiritual ecstasy. Shirdi, the sanctuary of Sai Baba, a saint revered by people of all faiths, was a testament to the power of faith and the universality of spiritual teachings.

As I reflect upon my soulful pilgrimage through India, I am filled with gratitude for the opportunity to have experienced the diverse and vibrant tapestry of spirituality that this land has to offer. The journey has been transformative, enriching my understanding of myself, the world around me, and the deeper meaning of life.

In sharing my experiences through this book, "Soulful Pilgrimage: Exploring Spiritual Journeys in India," I hope to inspire others to embark on their own spiritual quests, to discover the hidden treasures that lie within, and to embrace the diversity and richness of India's spiritual traditions. May this book serve as a guide and a companion for all those who seek to deepen their understanding of themselves and their connection with the divine.

Dr. Minakshi Bansal
Social Activist
Ahmedabad, Gujarat, Bharat

ᗡᗡᗡ

ONE

Varanasi: Where the Ganges Whispers Eternal Truths

Varanasi, a city that resonates with the rhythmic whispers of the Ganges, stands as an eternal testament to the intricate tapestry of life, death, and spirituality. With its labyrinthine alleyways, vibrant ghats, and a symphony of chanting that fills the air, Varanasi is a city where the past and present intertwine, where the mundane and the divine coexist.

As one wanders through the narrow lanes of Varanasi, the senses are overwhelmed by a kaleidoscope of sights, sounds, and smells. The aroma of incense mingles with the fragrance of spices, the rhythmic clanging of temple bells blends with the calls of street vendors, and the vibrant hues of sarees and dhotis dance amidst the muted tones of ancient buildings. It is a city that awakens the soul, inviting introspection and contemplation.

The heart of Varanasi lies along the banks of the sacred Ganges, a river revered as a goddess and a lifeline for millions. The ghats, a series of steps leading down to the water's edge, are the epicenter of the city's spiritual life. From dawn till dusk, the ghats are abuzz with activity, as devotees perform rituals, priests offer prayers, and pilgrims take a holy dip in the sacred waters. The ghats are a microcosm of life, where birth, death, and renewal are celebrated with equal fervor.

At the Manikarnika Ghat, the largest cremation ground in Varanasi, the cycle of life and death is starkly evident. Here, the mortal remains of loved ones are consigned to the flames, amidst the chanting of mantras and the wails of mourners. It is a poignant reminder of the impermanence of life, and the eternal journey of the soul. The smoke that rises from the pyres carries with it the hopes and aspirations of the departed, mingling with the prayers of the living.

In contrast to the somber atmosphere of Manikarnika Ghat, the Dashashwamedh Ghat is a vibrant hub of activity. Here, the evening aarti, a ritual offering of light and prayers, is a spectacle that attracts thousands of devotees and tourists alike. As the sun sets over the Ganges, the ghat comes alive with the sound of chanting, the aroma of incense, and the mesmerizing glow of oil lamps. It is a moment of collective devotion, where the individual merges with the divine.

Beyond the ghats, Varanasi's temples are a testament to the city's rich spiritual heritage. The Kashi Vishwanath Temple, dedicated to Lord Shiva, is the most revered shrine in Varanasi. The golden spire of the temple shimmers in the sunlight, beckoning devotees from far and wide. The temple complex is a labyrinth of narrow corridors, shrines, and courtyards, each with its own unique charm.

The Sankat Mochan Hanuman Temple, dedicated to Lord Hanuman, is another popular pilgrimage site in Varanasi. The temple is believed to have the power to remove obstacles and grant wishes. Devotees offer prayers and make offerings to the deity, seeking his blessings and protection.

As one delves deeper into Varanasi's spiritual landscape, one encounters a plethora of sadhus, ascetics who have renounced worldly possessions in pursuit of enlightenment. These saffron-clad figures, with their matted hair and ash-smeared bodies, are a common sight in Varanasi. They can be found meditating on the ghats, chanting mantras, or simply wandering the streets, lost in their own world.

The sadhus are a reminder of the diverse paths to spirituality, and the importance of introspection and detachment from material desires. Their presence adds to the mystical aura of Varanasi, making it a city where the seeker and the sought coexist.

Varanasi is not just a city of temples and ghats; it is also a center of learning and culture. The Banaras Hindu University, one of the oldest and largest universities in India, is located in Varanasi. The university has been a hub of intellectual and cultural activity for over a century, producing scholars, artists, and leaders in various fields.

The city's cultural scene is vibrant and diverse, with a rich tradition of music, dance, and theater. The classical music of Varanasi, known as Benarasi Gharana, is renowned for its soulful melodies and intricate rhythms. The city's dance forms, such as Kathak and Bharatnatyam, are a visual feast, showcasing the grace and elegance of Indian classical dance.

Varanasi's artisans are renowned for their exquisite craftsmanship, creating intricate silk sarees, brassware, and wooden toys. The city's markets are a treasure trove of handicrafts, offering a glimpse into the artistic traditions of the region.

The cuisine of Varanasi is a reflection of the city's diverse cultural influences. From the spicy street food to the elaborate thalis served in traditional restaurants, the culinary scene in Varanasi is a gastronomical adventure. The city's signature dish, the Benarasi paan, is a betel leaf preparation that is said to have originated in Varanasi.

While Varanasi is a city steeped in tradition, it is also a city that is embracing modernity. The city is witnessing a surge in tourism, with visitors from all over the world flocking to experience its unique charm. The government is also taking steps to improve infrastructure and amenities, making Varanasi a more accessible and comfortable destination for travelers.

However, the influx of tourists has also brought with it challenges, such as overcrowding, pollution, and commercialization. The delicate balance between preserving tradition and embracing modernity is a constant struggle for Varanasi.

Despite the challenges, Varanasi remains a city that continues to inspire and intrigue. It is a city that awakens the soul, challenges the mind, and nourishes the spirit. It is a city that whispers eternal truths, inviting us to delve deeper into the mysteries of life, death, and spirituality.

In conclusion, Varanasi is a city that defies definition. It is a city of contrasts, where the ancient and the modern, the sacred and the profane, the spiritual and the material coexist. It is a city that beckons the seeker, the wanderer, and the curious, offering a glimpse into the heart of India's spiritual heritage.

As the Ganges continues to flow, whispering its eternal truths, Varanasi stands as a timeless testament to the human spirit's quest for meaning and transcendence. It is a city that invites us to pause, reflect, and connect with our inner selves, reminding us of the eternal cycle of life, death, and rebirth.

ϷϷϷ

Varanasi, a symphony of life and death, where the Ganges whispers tales of eternity. The city's ghats echo with the rhythmic chants of prayers, inviting souls to immerse in the sacred waters and seek liberation. In the heart of this ancient city, the Kashi Vishwanath Temple stands as a beacon of devotion, its golden spire piercing the sky.

TWO

RISHIKESH: YOGA CAPITAL OF THE WORLD - FINDING INNER PEACE

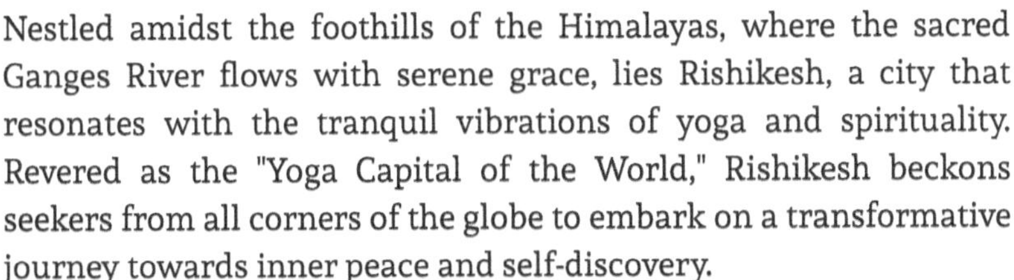

Nestled amidst the foothills of the Himalayas, where the sacred Ganges River flows with serene grace, lies Rishikesh, a city that resonates with the tranquil vibrations of yoga and spirituality. Revered as the "Yoga Capital of the World," Rishikesh beckons seekers from all corners of the globe to embark on a transformative journey towards inner peace and self-discovery.

Stepping into Rishikesh is akin to entering a sanctuary where the chaos of the outside world fades away, replaced by a soothing symphony of chanting, the gentle rustling of leaves, and the rhythmic flow of the Ganges. The city's air is imbued with an ethereal energy that permeates every nook and cranny, inviting visitors to slow down, breathe deeply, and reconnect with their inner essence.

The spiritual heart of Rishikesh lies in its numerous ashrams and yoga schools, each offering a unique path towards enlightenment. These sanctuaries of learning and practice are not mere institutions; they are vibrant communities where seekers from diverse backgrounds come together to delve into the profound wisdom of yoga, meditation, and philosophy.

Within the hallowed walls of these ashrams, the ancient teachings of yoga are brought to life, not as mere physical exercises, but as a holistic way of living. Asanas, or yoga postures, are practiced with mindfulness and reverence, each movement a conscious act of aligning the body, mind, and spirit. Pranayama, or breath control techniques, are taught as a means of harnessing the life force energy that flows through us, revitalizing the body and calming the mind.

Meditation, the cornerstone of spiritual practice, is cultivated as a means of transcending the limitations of the ego and experiencing the boundless nature of consciousness. In the serene atmosphere of Rishikesh, meditation becomes effortless, as the mind naturally settles into stillness, allowing for deeper insights and profound revelations to emerge.

The teachings of yoga are not confined to the ashram walls; they permeate the very fabric of life in Rishikesh. The city's vibrant markets are filled with shops selling yoga mats, malas, incense, and other spiritual paraphernalia. Cafes and restaurants offer wholesome vegetarian fare that nourishes the body and supports the yogic lifestyle.

The Ganges River, the lifeline of Rishikesh, is not merely a source of water; it is a sacred entity revered as a goddess. Pilgrims and tourists alike flock to its banks to take a dip in its holy waters, seeking purification and blessings. The ghats, or steps leading down to the river, are bustling with activity, as devotees perform rituals, priests chant mantras, and children splash around in joyful abandon.

The evening aarti, a ritual offering of light and prayers, is a spectacle that attracts thousands of spectators to the Parmarth Niketan ashram. As the sun sets over the Ganges, the ghat comes alive with the sound of chanting, the aroma of incense, and the mesmerizing glow of oil lamps. It is a moment of collective devotion, where the individual merges with the divine.

Beyond the ashrams and ghats, Rishikesh offers a wealth of natural beauty that soothes the soul and invigorates the senses. The city is surrounded by lush forests, rolling hills, and cascading waterfalls, providing ample opportunities for hiking, trekking, and nature walks.

The Beatles Ashram, once a retreat for the iconic band, is now a popular pilgrimage site for music lovers and spiritual seekers. The abandoned ashram, with its graffiti-covered walls and overgrown gardens, exudes a melancholic charm that invites contemplation and introspection.

Rishikesh is also a hub for adventure sports, offering activities such as white-water rafting, bungee jumping, and rock climbing. These adrenaline-pumping experiences provide a unique way to connect with nature and challenge oneself, pushing the boundaries of fear and self-doubt.

As the sun sets over Rishikesh, the city transforms into a tranquil haven, where the sounds of nature take center stage. The chirping of crickets, the gentle lapping of the Ganges, and the distant calls of birds create a symphony that lulls one into a state of deep relaxation.

The evenings in Rishikesh are often spent in satsang, or spiritual gatherings, where seekers come together to chant, meditate, and listen to discourses by enlightened masters. These gatherings provide a platform for sharing experiences, seeking guidance, and fostering a sense of community among like-minded individuals.

For those seeking solitude and introspection, Rishikesh offers numerous secluded spots where one can simply be. Whether it's meditating by the riverbank, journaling in a quiet cafe, or simply gazing at the stars, Rishikesh provides ample opportunities to disconnect from the external world and reconnect with one's inner self.

The transformative power of Rishikesh lies not only in its teachings and practices but also in its ability to foster a sense of belonging and connection. The city attracts seekers from all walks of life, creating a melting pot of cultures, beliefs, and perspectives.

In this diverse and inclusive environment, one is encouraged to shed preconceived notions and embrace a spirit of openness and curiosity. Interactions with fellow seekers from different backgrounds can lead to profound insights, unexpected friendships, and a broadening of one's worldview.

The journey towards inner peace is not a linear one; it is a continuous process of self-discovery and growth. Rishikesh provides the ideal environment for this journey, offering a multitude of tools, teachings, and experiences that support one's spiritual evolution.

Whether it's through the practice of yoga, meditation, or simply spending time in nature, Rishikesh has a way of unlocking one's hidden potential and revealing the true essence of being. The city's tranquil ambiance, coupled with the wisdom of its teachers and the support of its community, creates a fertile ground for transformation to occur.

In conclusion, Rishikesh is not just a city; it is a spiritual oasis that offers solace, inspiration, and a path towards inner peace. Its rich tapestry of yoga, meditation, philosophy, and natural beauty weaves a magical spell that captivates the hearts and minds of all who enter its embrace.

As the Ganges continues to flow, carrying with it the prayers and aspirations of countless seekers, Rishikesh stands as a beacon of hope, reminding us that inner peace is not a distant dream, but a tangible reality that can be attained through dedication, practice, and an unwavering faith in the transformative power of yoga.

Rishikesh, where the Himalayas embrace the Ganges, a sanctuary for seekers of inner peace. The tranquil ashrams and yoga schools offer a path to self-discovery through ancient wisdom and mindful practices. Let the rhythmic flow of the river and the gentle rustling of leaves guide you towards serenity.

THREE

HARIDWAR: GATEWAY TO THE GODS - A DIP IN HOLY WATERS

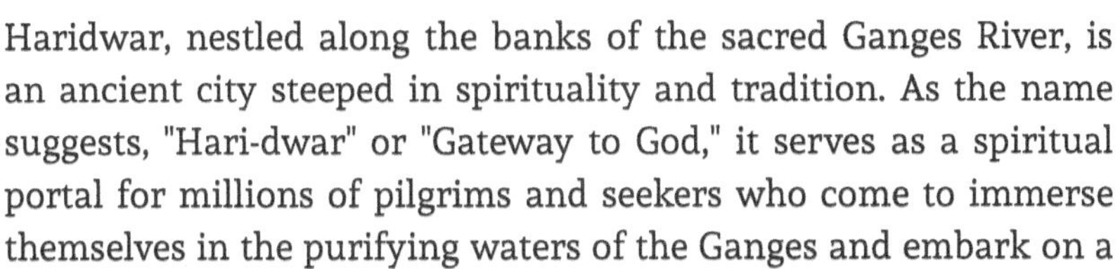

Haridwar, nestled along the banks of the sacred Ganges River, is an ancient city steeped in spirituality and tradition. As the name suggests, "Hari-dwar" or "Gateway to God," it serves as a spiritual portal for millions of pilgrims and seekers who come to immerse themselves in the purifying waters of the Ganges and embark on a transformative journey.

The city's spiritual significance is palpable in every corner, from the bustling ghats where devotees gather for ritualistic bathing to the numerous temples and ashrams that dot the landscape. Haridwar's vibrant atmosphere is a testament to the enduring power of faith and the human yearning for connection with the divine.

Har Ki Pauri, the most sacred ghat in Haridwar, is the epicenter of spiritual activity. Here, the Ganges flows with a gentle force, inviting devotees to take a dip in its holy waters. The ghat is a mesmerizing sight, especially during the evening aarti, when thousands of oil lamps are lit and offered to the river goddess, Ganga. The air is filled with the sound of chanting, the aroma of incense, and the collective energy of devotion.

The Kumbh Mela, a grand religious festival held every twelve years in Haridwar, is a testament to the city's spiritual significance. Millions of pilgrims from all over the world converge on Haridwar during this auspicious occasion to take a holy dip in the Ganges and seek blessings from the divine. The Kumbh Mela is a sight to behold, with its vast crowds, colorful processions, and vibrant displays of faith.

Beyond Har Ki Pauri, Haridwar offers a wealth of spiritual experiences for the seeker. The Mansa Devi Temple, perched atop the Bilwa Parvat hill, is dedicated to Goddess Mansa, the fulfiller of wishes. Devotees throng to the temple to offer prayers and seek blessings, hoping for their desires to be granted.

The Chandi Devi Temple, another revered shrine in Haridwar, is dedicated to Goddess Chandi, a fierce manifestation of Shakti, the divine feminine energy. The temple is believed to have been established by Adi Shankaracharya, a revered philosopher and saint, in the 8th century.

The Daksha Mahadev Temple, also known as Daksheshwar Mahadev Temple, is dedicated to Lord Shiva. The temple is believed to be the site where King Daksha Prajapati, the father of Sati, performed a yagna, or sacrificial ritual, that led to a series of events culminating in Sati's self-immolation and Lord Shiva's wrathful dance of destruction.

Haridwar's numerous ashrams offer a serene environment for spiritual practice and self-reflection. These sanctuaries of learning and devotion provide a space for individuals to delve deeper into their spiritual journey, guided by experienced teachers and mentors.

The Sapt Rishi Ashram, or the Ashram of the Seven Sages, is a revered institution in Haridwar. It is believed to be the spot where seven sages, Kashyapa, Vashishtha, Atri, Vishwamitra, Jamadagni, Bharadwaja, and Gautama, meditated on the banks of the Ganges. The ashram offers courses in yoga, meditation, and Vedanta philosophy, attracting seekers from all over the world.

The Shantikunj Ashram, established by the All World Gayatri Pariwar, is a modern ashram that focuses on social reform and spiritual upliftment. The ashram offers various programs and workshops aimed at promoting individual and societal transformation.

Haridwar's spiritual landscape is not limited to temples and ashrams. The city's vibrant markets are filled with shops selling religious paraphernalia, Ayurvedic medicines, and traditional handicrafts. The aroma of incense fills the air, mingling with the fragrance of spices and the sounds of devotional music.

The cuisine of Haridwar is a reflection of the city's spiritual ethos. Most restaurants and eateries offer vegetarian fare, with a focus on fresh, locally sourced ingredients. The city's street food is a culinary adventure in itself, with a wide array of savory snacks and sweets to tantalize the taste buds.

While Haridwar is primarily a spiritual destination, it also offers a glimpse into the region's rich cultural heritage. The city's architecture is a blend of ancient and modern, with traditional temples and havelis coexisting with contemporary buildings.

The Ganga Aarti at Har Ki Pauri is a nightly ritual that showcases the city's cultural traditions. The aarti is a mesmerizing spectacle, with priests chanting mantras and waving oil lamps in synchronized movements, creating a mesmerizing symphony of light and sound.

The Haridwar Kumbh Mela is not just a religious gathering; it is also a cultural extravaganza. The mela features various cultural programs, including music and dance performances, exhibitions, and seminars. It is a platform for artists and artisans from all over India to showcase their talent and creativity.

Haridwar's natural beauty adds another dimension to its allure. The city is surrounded by lush forests, rolling hills, and the majestic Ganges River. The Rajaji National Park, located on the outskirts of Haridwar, is home to a diverse range of flora and fauna, including elephants, tigers, and leopards.

The Chilla Wildlife Sanctuary, situated on the banks of the Ganges, is a haven for birdwatchers, with over 315 species of birds recorded in the sanctuary. The Neelkanth Mahadev Temple, nestled amidst the Shivalik hills, is a popular pilgrimage site and a scenic spot offering panoramic views of the surrounding landscape.

Haridwar's spiritual and cultural significance has made it a popular destination for tourists from all over the world. The city's tourism industry has grown rapidly in recent years, with a wide range of accommodation options catering to different budgets and preferences.

The influx of tourists has also brought with it challenges, such as overcrowding, pollution, and commercialization. However, the city's authorities are taking steps to address these issues, with initiatives aimed at promoting sustainable tourism and preserving the city's unique character.

In conclusion, Haridwar is a city that embodies the essence of

India's spiritual heritage. It is a place where the ancient and the modern, the sacred and the profane, the spiritual and the material coexist in harmonious balance.

Whether it is seeking blessings at the Har Ki Pauri ghat, exploring the city's numerous temples and ashrams, or simply immersing oneself in the vibrant atmosphere, Haridwar offers a unique and transformative experience for the seeker.

As the Ganges continues to flow, carrying with it the hopes and aspirations of millions, Haridwar stands as a timeless testament to the enduring power of faith and the human quest for spiritual enlightenment.

Haridwar, the gateway to the gods, a place where the sacred Ganges purifies and rejuvenates. Witness the mesmerizing spectacle of the Kumbh Mela, where millions gather in a vibrant display of faith and devotion. Take a dip in the holy waters and let the divine energy wash over you.

FOUR

AMRITSAR: GOLDEN TEMPLE'S DIVINE EMBRACE - SIKH SPIRITUALITY

Amritsar, a city steeped in history and spirituality, is synonymous with the Golden Temple, a beacon of Sikh devotion and a symbol of unity and equality. The city's very name, derived from "Amrit Sarovar," the pool of nectar surrounding the temple, evokes the essence of its sacredness and the transformative power it holds for millions of devotees.

Stepping into the Golden Temple complex is akin to entering a realm of divine serenity and grace. The shimmering golden facade of the Harmandir Sahib, the sanctum sanctorum, reflects the sunlight, creating an ethereal glow that mesmerizes and uplifts the soul. The temple's architecture, a harmonious blend of Hindu and Islamic styles, is a testament to the Sikh philosophy of inclusivity and acceptance.

The Amrit Sarovar, the sacred pool surrounding the temple, is believed to possess healing properties. Devotees from all walks of life take a dip in its holy waters, seeking physical and spiritual purification. The pool's placid surface reflects the golden temple, creating a mesmerizing illusion of the temple floating on water.

The causeway leading to the Harmandir Sahib is a symbolic journey towards the divine. As one walks across the marble bridge, the mind gradually stills, and the heart opens to the spiritual vibrations that permeate the air. The sound of the Guru Granth Sahib, the Sikh holy scripture, being recited from within the temple, adds to the serene ambiance.

The Harmandir Sahib, the heart of the Golden Temple complex, is a place of profound reverence and devotion. The Guru Granth Sahib, installed on a raised platform under a canopy adorned with precious stones, is the focal point of worship. Devotees circumambulate the sanctum sanctorum, offering prayers and seeking blessings from the Guru.

The interior of the Harmandir Sahib is adorned with intricate gold and silver work, creating a dazzling spectacle that inspires awe and wonder. The walls are inlaid with precious stones and the ceiling is adorned with frescoes depicting scenes from Sikh history and mythology. The ambiance is one of tranquility and devotion, where the mind is naturally drawn towards contemplation and prayer.

The Golden Temple complex is not just a place of worship; it is a vibrant hub of community life. The langar, or community kitchen, is a testament to the Sikh principle of seva, or selfless service. Here, volunteers prepare and serve free meals to thousands of people every day, regardless of their caste, creed, or social status.

The langar is a powerful symbol of equality and compassion, where everyone is welcome to partake in the simple yet nourishing food. The act of serving and eating together fosters a sense of community and shared humanity, transcending social barriers and promoting unity.

The Akal Takht, the highest seat of temporal authority in Sikhism, is located opposite the Harmandir Sahib. The Akal Takht is a symbol of Sikh sovereignty and justice, where important decisions regarding the Sikh community are taken. It is also a place of learning and discourse, where scholars and theologians discuss and interpret Sikh scriptures and traditions.

The Golden Temple complex is not just a religious site; it is also a living museum of Sikh history and culture. The Central Sikh Museum, located within the complex, houses a vast collection of artifacts, manuscripts, and paintings that chronicle the Sikh journey from its inception to the present day.

The museum's exhibits provide a glimpse into the lives of the Sikh Gurus, their teachings, and the struggles and triumphs of the Sikh community. The museum also showcases the rich artistic and cultural heritage of the Sikhs, with displays of traditional clothing, weaponry, and musical instruments.

The Golden Temple complex is a place of immense historical significance. It has witnessed numerous events that have shaped the course of Sikh history, including the martyrdom of Guru Arjan Dev Ji, the fifth Sikh Guru, and the Operation Blue Star, a military operation carried out by the Indian government in 1984.

Despite the turbulent times it has witnessed, the Golden Temple remains a symbol of resilience, hope, and faith. It continues to inspire millions of people around the world, attracting pilgrims and tourists alike who come to experience its unique spiritual ambiance and learn about the Sikh way of life.

Amritsar, as the home of the Golden Temple, is a city that pulsates with the rhythm of Sikh spirituality. The city's streets are lined with shops selling religious paraphernalia, traditional clothing, and local delicacies. The aroma of spices and incense fills the air, creating a sensory experience that is both invigorating and calming.

The Jallianwala Bagh, a public garden located near the Golden Temple, is a poignant reminder of the sacrifices made by the Sikhs in their struggle for freedom. The garden was the site of a massacre in 1919, where hundreds of unarmed civilians were killed by British troops. The bullet marks on the walls of the garden are a chilling reminder of the brutality of the colonial era.

The Wagah Border, located on the outskirts of Amritsar, is a popular tourist attraction where the daily border closing ceremony between India and Pakistan takes place. The ceremony, a display of military pageantry and patriotism, is a spectacle that attracts large crowds of spectators.

Amritsar's culinary scene is a reflection of the city's rich cultural heritage. The city is famous for its Amritsari kulcha, a type of flatbread stuffed with potatoes and spices, and its Amritsari fish, a delicacy made with marinated fish fried in a batter of gram flour and spices. The city's street food is a culinary adventure, with a wide array of savory snacks and sweets to tantalize the taste buds.

Amritsar is a city that seamlessly blends tradition with modernity. While it is deeply rooted in its spiritual and cultural heritage, it is also a thriving urban center with a burgeoning economy. The city's infrastructure is well-developed, with modern amenities and facilities catering to the needs of its residents and visitors.

Amritsar's hospitality is legendary. The city's people are warm, welcoming, and always eager to share their culture and traditions with visitors. The spirit of seva, or selfless service, is ingrained in the city's ethos, making it a place where one feels truly at home.

In conclusion, Amritsar is a city that encapsulates the essence of Sikh spirituality. It is a place where faith, history, and culture converge, creating a unique and unforgettable experience for all who visit. The Golden Temple, with its divine embrace, is the heart and soul of Amritsar, drawing people from all walks of life to its sacred precincts.

As the city continues to evolve and adapt to the changing times, it remains steadfast in its commitment to preserving its rich heritage and upholding the values of equality, compassion, and service. Amritsar is a testament to the enduring power of faith and the human spirit's quest for meaning and transcendence.

ppp

Amritsar, the radiant heart of Sikh spirituality, where the Golden Temple's golden glow illuminates the soul. Experience the warmth of the langar, where selfless service and the spirit of sharing nourish the body and spirit. The Golden Temple, a symbol of unity and equality, beckons all to its sacred embrace.

FIVE

BODH GAYA: MAHABODHI TEMPLE – WHERE BUDDHA FOUND ENLIGHTENMENT

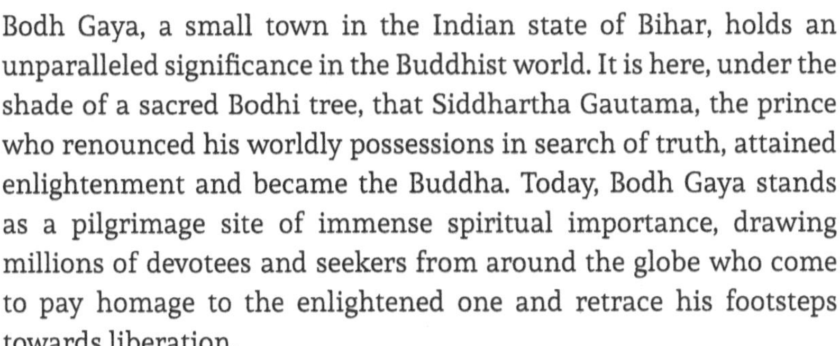

Bodh Gaya, a small town in the Indian state of Bihar, holds an unparalleled significance in the Buddhist world. It is here, under the shade of a sacred Bodhi tree, that Siddhartha Gautama, the prince who renounced his worldly possessions in search of truth, attained enlightenment and became the Buddha. Today, Bodh Gaya stands as a pilgrimage site of immense spiritual importance, drawing millions of devotees and seekers from around the globe who come to pay homage to the enlightened one and retrace his footsteps towards liberation.

At the heart of Bodh Gaya lies the Mahabodhi Temple, a UNESCO World Heritage Site and a magnificent testament to the enduring legacy of the Buddha. The temple complex, with its soaring spires, intricate carvings, and serene atmosphere, exudes an aura of tranquility and reverence that instantly transports visitors to a realm of spiritual awakening.

The Mahabodhi Temple's origins date back to the 3rd century BCE when Emperor Ashoka, a fervent patron of Buddhism, erected a shrine to mark the spot where the Buddha attained enlightenment. Over the centuries, the temple underwent several renovations and expansions, culminating in the present-day structure that stands as a beacon of Buddhist devotion.

The temple's architecture is a harmonious blend of various styles, reflecting the diverse cultural influences that have shaped Buddhism over the centuries. The main tower, or shikhara, rises majestically towards the heavens, its gilded surface shimmering in the sunlight. The intricate carvings that adorn the temple's walls depict scenes from the Buddha's life, his teachings, and the rich tapestry of Buddhist mythology.

The sanctum sanctorum of the Mahabodhi Temple houses a colossal statue of the Buddha in a seated posture, his hands resting in the dhyana mudra, the gesture of meditation. The statue's serene countenance and gentle smile radiate an aura of peace and compassion that envelops the entire temple complex.

The Bodhi tree, under which the Buddha attained enlightenment, is the most sacred site in Bodh Gaya. A descendant of the original tree, it stands as a living symbol of the Buddha's awakening and the potential for enlightenment that resides within each of us. Devotees circumambulate the tree, offering prayers and seeking blessings, their hearts filled with gratitude and reverence.

The Vajrasana, or Diamond Throne, is another sacred site within the temple complex. It is believed to be the exact spot where the Buddha sat in meditation for forty-nine days, ultimately achieving enlightenment. The Vajrasana is a place of profound spiritual significance, where pilgrims come to meditate and connect with the Buddha's energy.

The Mahabodhi Temple complex is not just a place of worship; it is a vibrant hub of Buddhist activity and learning. The temple premises house several monasteries and meditation centers where monks and nuns from various traditions reside and practice. These monastic communities play a vital role in preserving and propagating the Buddha's teachings, offering guidance and support to seekers on their spiritual journey.

The temple complex also hosts numerous cultural and religious events throughout the year, attracting a diverse array of visitors from all corners of the globe. The annual Bodh Gaya Enlightenment Day celebrations are a major highlight, drawing thousands of pilgrims who come to participate in prayers, meditation sessions, and cultural programs.

The teachings of the Buddha, as enshrined in the Mahabodhi Temple, continue to inspire and guide millions of people around the world. The Four Noble Truths, the Eightfold Path, and the concept of mindfulness are just some of the profound insights that the Buddha offered to humanity, providing a roadmap towards a life of peace, compassion, and wisdom.

Bodh Gaya, with its rich history, sacred sites, and vibrant spiritual community, is a place that awakens the soul and nourishes the spirit. It is a place where one can connect with the essence of Buddhism, delve deeper into its teachings, and embark on a transformative journey towards self-discovery and enlightenment.

The Mahabodhi Temple, as the epicenter of Buddhist devotion in Bodh Gaya, stands as a beacon of hope and inspiration for all who seek to tread the path of the Buddha. Its serene ambiance, coupled with the wisdom of its teachings and the support of its monastic community, creates a fertile ground for spiritual growth and transformation.

In conclusion, Bodh Gaya is a place of immense spiritual significance, a place where the Buddha's legacy lives on, inspiring generations of seekers to embark on a journey towards enlightenment. The Mahabodhi Temple, with its grandeur, history, and serene atmosphere, is a testament to the enduring power of the Buddha's teachings and the universal appeal of his message of peace, compassion, and wisdom.

As the Bodhi tree continues to flourish, its leaves rustling in the gentle breeze, Bodh Gaya remains a sacred haven for all who seek to connect with their inner Buddha and awaken to the true nature of reality.

ᛒᛒᛒ

Bodh Gaya, the sacred ground where Buddha's enlightenment blossomed. The Mahabodhi Temple, a majestic testament to his legacy, invites contemplation and introspection. Sit under the Bodhi tree, where the enlightened one found liberation, and let the wisdom of his teachings guide your path.

SIX

DHARAMSHALA: DALAI LAMA'S ABODE - TIBETAN BUDDHISM IN EXILE

Dharamshala, nestled amidst the breathtaking Dhauladhar mountain range in the Indian state of Himachal Pradesh, is not merely a picturesque hill station; it is a sanctuary of Tibetan Buddhism in exile, a place where the teachings of compassion, wisdom, and non-violence find refuge and resonance.

The city's association with Tibetan Buddhism began in 1959, when His Holiness the 14th Dalai Lama, along with thousands of Tibetan refugees, sought asylum in India following the Chinese occupation of Tibet. Dharamshala, with its serene ambiance and welcoming community, became the Dalai Lama's abode and the seat of the Tibetan government-in-exile.

Today, Dharamshala is a thriving hub of Tibetan culture, spirituality, and activism. The city's streets are lined with Tibetan shops and restaurants, prayer flags flutter in the breeze, and the air is filled with the sound of chanting and the aroma of incense. It is a place where the Tibetan identity is preserved, nurtured, and celebrated.

The Tsuglagkhang Complex, the Dalai Lama's official residence and the spiritual heart of Dharamshala, is a place of immense significance for Tibetans and Buddhists alike. The complex houses the Namgyal Monastery, the personal monastery of the Dalai Lama, where monks engage in daily prayers, rituals, and study of Buddhist scriptures.

The Tsuglagkhang Temple, the main temple within the complex, is a magnificent structure adorned with intricate murals, thangkas (Tibetan scroll paintings), and statues of Buddhist deities. The temple's serene atmosphere and the presence of the Dalai Lama's throne create an aura of reverence and devotion.

The temple complex also houses the Tibet Museum, a repository of Tibetan history, culture, and art. The museum's exhibits chronicle the Tibetan struggle for freedom, the Dalai Lama's life and teachings, and the rich cultural heritage of Tibet. It is a place where visitors can gain a deeper understanding of Tibet's past, present, and future.

The Library of Tibetan Works and Archives, located within the Tsuglagkhang Complex, is a treasure trove of Tibetan literature, manuscripts, and historical documents. The library's collection is a testament to the rich intellectual and spiritual traditions of Tibet, preserving centuries of knowledge and wisdom for future generations.

Beyond the Tsuglagkhang Complex, Dharamshala offers a wealth of spiritual experiences for the seeker. The Norbulingka Institute, located on the outskirts of the city, is a center for the preservation and promotion of Tibetan arts and crafts. The institute's workshops offer training in traditional Tibetan arts such as thangka painting, wood carving, and metalwork, providing a livelihood for Tibetan refugees and preserving their cultural heritage.

The Gyuto Tantric Monastery, located near Dharamshala, is a renowned center for the study and practice of Tantric Buddhism. The monastery's monks are known for their deep meditative practices and their multiphonic chanting, a unique form of chanting where a single vocalist produces multiple tones simultaneously.

The Tibetan Institute of Performing Arts (TIPA), established by the Dalai Lama in 1959, is dedicated to the preservation and promotion of Tibetan performing arts. The institute offers training in traditional Tibetan music, dance, and theater, providing a platform for Tibetan artists to showcase their talent and creativity.

Dharamshala's spiritual landscape is not limited to monasteries and institutes. The city's vibrant markets are filled with Tibetan handicrafts, prayer flags, incense, and other spiritual paraphernalia. The aroma of Tibetan tea and momos (dumplings) wafts through the air, inviting visitors to savor the flavors of Tibetan cuisine.

The annual Tibetan New Year, or Losar, is a major festival celebrated with great enthusiasm in Dharamshala. The festivities include traditional dances, music performances, and the burning of juniper incense to ward off evil spirits. It is a time for Tibetans to come together, celebrate their culture, and renew their hopes for a free Tibet.

The Dalai Lama's teachings of compassion, non-violence, and the pursuit of inner peace have resonated with people from all walks of life. His message of hope and resilience in the face of adversity has inspired millions around the world. Dharamshala, as the Dalai

Lama's abode, serves as a beacon of hope for Tibetans and a reminder of the importance of preserving one's cultural identity and spiritual values.

The city's welcoming community and its commitment to social justice have made it a haven for refugees and seekers from all over the world. The Dalai Lama's teachings on interfaith dialogue and the importance of building bridges between different cultures and religions have fostered an environment of tolerance and understanding in Dharamshala.

In conclusion, Dharamshala is a city that embodies the spirit of Tibetan Buddhism in exile. It is a place where the teachings of compassion, wisdom, and non-violence find refuge and resonance. The city's vibrant cultural scene, its spiritual institutions, and its commitment to social justice make it a unique and inspiring destination for seekers from all walks of life.

As the Dalai Lama continues to inspire millions with his message of hope and compassion, Dharamshala stands as a testament to the enduring power of the human spirit and the importance of preserving cultural heritage and spiritual values in the face of adversity.

ᛈᛈᛈ

Dharamshala, a haven for Tibetan Buddhism in exile, where the Dalai Lama's compassionate presence radiates peace. Explore the Tsuglagkhang Complex, a repository of Tibetan culture and spirituality, and let the serenity of the mountains inspire your journey towards inner peace.

SEVEN

TIRUPATI: LORD VENKATESWARA'S BLESSINGS - A SACRED HILLTOP SHRINE

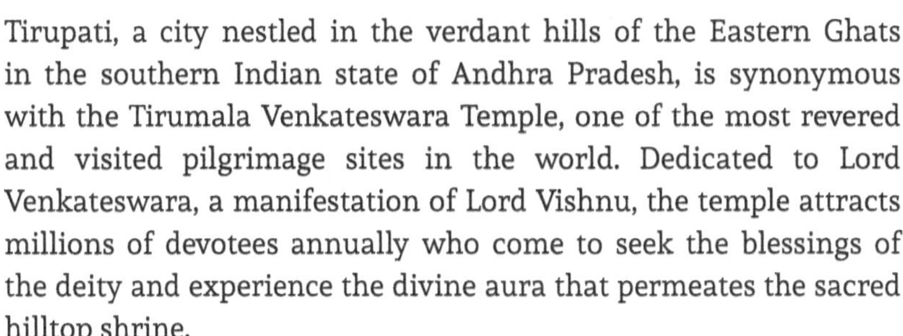

Tirupati, a city nestled in the verdant hills of the Eastern Ghats in the southern Indian state of Andhra Pradesh, is synonymous with the Tirumala Venkateswara Temple, one of the most revered and visited pilgrimage sites in the world. Dedicated to Lord Venkateswara, a manifestation of Lord Vishnu, the temple attracts millions of devotees annually who come to seek the blessings of the deity and experience the divine aura that permeates the sacred hilltop shrine.

The journey to Tirumala, the hill on which the temple is situated, is an arduous yet spiritually uplifting experience. Pilgrims can either trek up the steep slopes, a physically demanding but spiritually rewarding endeavor, or opt for the convenience of buses and taxis that ply the winding roads. As one ascends the hill, the air grows cooler, the scenery becomes more breathtaking, and a sense of anticipation and reverence fills the heart.

The Tirumala Venkateswara Temple complex is a sprawling architectural marvel, a testament to the devotion and craftsmanship of generations of artisans and architects. The temple's main entrance, the Mahadwaram, is a towering gateway adorned with intricate carvings and sculptures of deities and mythological figures. The gopuram, or tower, of the temple rises majestically above the surrounding landscape, its golden kalasam, or finial, glinting in the sunlight.

The sanctum sanctorum of the temple houses the idol of Lord Venkateswara, also known as Balaji, a deity revered for his benevolence and compassion. The idol, believed to be self-manifested, is adorned with precious ornaments and garments, and is a sight to behold. Devotees offer prayers, make offerings, and seek blessings from the Lord, their hearts filled with gratitude and devotion.

The temple complex is a labyrinth of mandapams, or pillared halls, each with its unique purpose and significance. The Ranga Mandapam, a vast hall with intricately carved pillars, is where devotees wait in queues for their turn to have a darshan, or glimpse, of the Lord. The Vimana Venkateswara shrine, located behind the main sanctum, houses a smaller idol of the Lord, which is believed to be even more powerful than the main idol.

The temple complex also houses several other shrines dedicated to various deities, including Goddess Padmavati, the consort of Lord Venkateswara, and Lord Ganesha, the remover of obstacles. The temple's architecture is a harmonious blend of Dravidian and Vijayanagara styles, with intricate carvings, ornate pillars, and majestic gopurams that leave visitors spellbound.

The Tirumala Venkateswara Temple is not just a place of worship; it is a bustling hub of religious and cultural activity. The temple administration, the Tirumala Tirupati Devasthanams (TTD), is a well-oiled machine that manages the temple's day-to-day operations, ensuring a smooth and seamless experience for the millions of devotees who visit each year.

The TTD offers a range of services for pilgrims, including accommodation, food, and transportation. The temple kitchen, the largest in the world, prepares and serves thousands of meals every day, ensuring that no devotee goes hungry. The temple also has a hospital, a library, and a museum, catering to the diverse needs of its visitors.

The temple's annual Brahmotsavam festival, a nine-day extravaganza, is a sight to behold. The festival features a series of elaborate processions, cultural performances, and religious rituals, attracting devotees from all over the world. The Garuda Seva, a procession where the Lord is carried on the shoulders of his celestial mount, Garuda, is a major highlight of the festival.

The Tirupati Laddu, a sweet offering made of gram flour, sugar, and ghee, is synonymous with the Tirumala Venkateswara Temple. The laddu, prepared in the temple kitchen, is considered to be prasadam, or blessed food, and is highly sought after by devotees. The TTD has a dedicated laddu counter where pilgrims can purchase this delectable treat.

The temple's economic impact on the region is immense. Tirupati, as a pilgrimage town, thrives on the influx of devotees, with numerous hotels, restaurants, and shops catering to their needs. The TTD, as the custodian of the temple, plays a crucial role in the region's economy, generating employment and contributing to the development of infrastructure and amenities.

The temple's social impact is equally significant. The TTD runs several charitable initiatives, including educational institutions, hospitals, and orphanages, providing much-needed support to the underprivileged sections of society. The temple also promotes religious harmony and interfaith dialogue, fostering a sense of unity and brotherhood among people of different faiths.

The Tirumala Venkateswara Temple, with its rich history, magnificent architecture, and spiritual significance, is a testament to the enduring power of faith and devotion. It is a place where the human spirit soars, where the heart finds solace, and where the soul connects with the divine.

As the pilgrims continue to flock to Tirupati, their hearts filled with hope and devotion, the Tirumala Venkateswara Temple stands tall, a beacon of spirituality and a symbol of India's rich cultural heritage.

ppp

Tirupati, a hilltop shrine where Lord Venkateswara's blessings shower upon devotees. Embark on a pilgrimage to this sacred abode, where the air is filled with the fragrance of devotion and the chants of pilgrims seeking divine grace.

EIGHT

RAMESHWARAM: RAMANATHASWAMY TEMPLE – SOUTHERNMOST JYOTIRLINGA

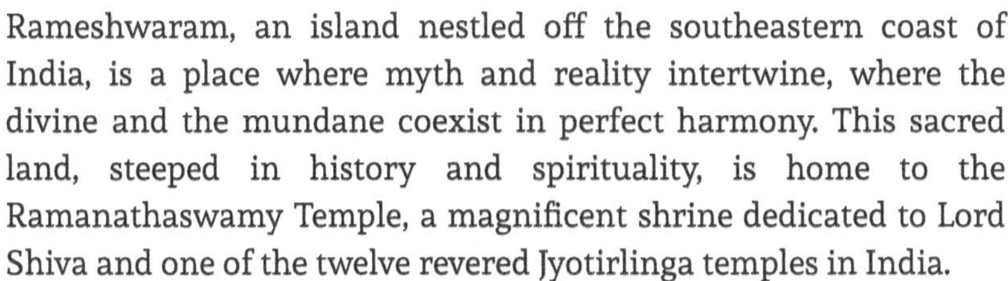

Rameshwaram, an island nestled off the southeastern coast of India, is a place where myth and reality intertwine, where the divine and the mundane coexist in perfect harmony. This sacred land, steeped in history and spirituality, is home to the Ramanathaswamy Temple, a magnificent shrine dedicated to Lord Shiva and one of the twelve revered Jyotirlinga temples in India.

The Ramanathaswamy Temple, with its towering gopurams (gateway towers), sprawling corridors, and intricately carved pillars, is an architectural marvel that leaves visitors spellbound. The temple's grandeur and serenity create an atmosphere of reverence and devotion, drawing pilgrims and seekers from all corners of the globe.

The temple's sanctum sanctorum houses the Jyotirlinga, a representation of Lord Shiva as a pillar of light. The Jyotirlinga is believed to be a self-manifested form of Shiva, radiating divine energy and granting blessings to devotees. Pilgrims offer prayers, perform rituals, and seek blessings from the Lord, their hearts filled with gratitude and reverence.

The Ramanathaswamy Temple is not just a place of worship; it is a treasure trove of history and mythology. The temple is believed to have been established by Lord Rama, the seventh avatar of Lord Vishnu, after his victorious return from Lanka. According to legend, Lord Rama, along with his wife Sita and brother Lakshmana, performed a ritual to absolve himself of the sin of killing Ravana, the demon king of Lanka.

The temple's corridors are adorned with murals and sculptures depicting scenes from the Ramayana, the epic that narrates the story of Lord Rama. The temple also houses several shrines dedicated to various deities, including Goddess Parvathavardhini, the consort of Lord Shiva, and Lord Ganesha, the remover of obstacles.

One of the unique features of the Ramanathaswamy Temple is its twenty-two sacred wells, known as theerthams. These wells, located within the temple complex, are believed to possess healing properties. Pilgrims take a dip in these wells, believing that the water will cleanse them of their sins and ailments. The theerthams are also believed to have originated from the arrows shot by Lord Rama to quench the thirst of Sita.

The Agni Theertham, the sea surrounding Rameshwaram, is considered to be the most sacred of all the theerthams. Pilgrims take a dip in the sea before entering the temple, believing that it will purify their body and soul. The Agni Theertham is also associated with the story of Lord Rama, who is believed to have offered prayers to the sea god before constructing the bridge to Lanka.

The Ramanathaswamy Temple is not just a religious site; it is also a cultural hub. The temple hosts several festivals and cultural events throughout the year, attracting a diverse array of visitors. The Maha Shivaratri festival, celebrated in honor of Lord Shiva, is a major event that draws thousands of pilgrims to Rameshwaram.

The temple's architecture, a blend of Dravidian and Vijayanagara styles, is a testament to the rich cultural heritage of the region. The temple's towering gopurams, intricately carved pillars, and sprawling corridors are a visual feast for the eyes. The temple's musical pillars, which produce different sounds when struck, are a marvel of ancient engineering.

The Ramanathaswamy Temple's spiritual and cultural significance has made it a popular pilgrimage destination for centuries. Pilgrims from all over India and beyond come to Rameshwaram to seek the blessings of Lord Shiva and experience the divine aura that permeates the sacred island.

The town of Rameshwaram, with its narrow lanes, colorful houses, and bustling markets, offers a glimpse into the local way of life. The town's economy thrives on tourism, with numerous hotels, restaurants, and shops catering to the needs of the pilgrims.

The Pamban Bridge, a cantilever bridge that connects Rameshwaram to mainland India, is a marvel of engineering and a popular tourist attraction. The bridge offers breathtaking views of the sea and the surrounding landscape.

The Dhanushkodi Beach, located at the southeastern tip of Rameshwaram, is a pristine stretch of sand known for its natural beauty and tranquility. The beach is a popular spot for swimming, sunbathing, and birdwatching.

Rameshwaram's natural beauty, coupled with its spiritual and cultural significance, makes it a unique and unforgettable destination. The island's pristine beaches, crystal-clear waters, and lush greenery provide a serene backdrop for spiritual contemplation and relaxation.

In conclusion, Rameshwaram is a place where the divine and the mundane converge, where faith and history intertwine, and where the human spirit soars. The Ramanathaswamy Temple, with its grandeur, history, and spiritual significance, is a testament to the enduring power of faith and the human quest for spiritual enlightenment.

As the waves of the Indian Ocean continue to lap against the shores of Rameshwaram, the Ramanathaswamy Temple stands tall, a beacon of hope and a symbol of India's rich cultural heritage.

ᐁᐁᐁ

Rameshwaram, an island where Lord Rama's legend echoes through the ages. The Ramanathaswamy Temple, a magnificent architectural marvel, stands as a testament to his devotion to Lord Shiva. Immerse yourself in the sacred waters of the theerthams and experience the divine energy that permeates this island.

NINE

MADURAI: MEENAKSHI AMMAN TEMPLE – A DRAVIDIAN ARCHITECTURAL MARVEL

Madurai, an ancient city in the heart of Tamil Nadu, is synonymous with the Meenakshi Amman Temple, a sprawling complex that stands as a testament to the rich cultural and architectural heritage of the region. The temple, dedicated to Goddess Meenakshi, a form of Parvati, and her consort, Sundareswarar, a form of Shiva, is not merely a place of worship; it is a living monument that encapsulates the essence of Dravidian art, architecture, and spirituality.

Stepping into the Meenakshi Amman Temple complex is akin to entering a different world, a world where myth and reality intertwine, where the divine and the mundane coexist in perfect harmony. The temple's towering gopurams, or gateway towers, adorned with a kaleidoscope of sculptures depicting gods, goddesses, demons, and celestial beings, beckon visitors into a realm of wonder and awe.

The temple complex, spread over 14 acres, is a labyrinth of mandapams, or pillared halls, each with its unique charm and significance. The Meenakshi Nayakkar Mandapam, a thousand-pillared hall, is a masterpiece of Dravidian architecture, with each pillar adorned with intricate carvings depicting mythological scenes and figures. The hall's acoustics are legendary, with the sound of a single clap reverberating through the entire space.

The Aayiram Kaal Mandapam, another thousand-pillared hall, is dedicated to Lord Nataraja, the cosmic dancer. The hall's pillars are adorned with sculptures of Nataraja in various dance poses, showcasing the grace and dynamism of this iconic deity.

The Golden Lotus Tank, a sacred pool located within the temple complex, is a place of ritual purification. Devotees take a dip in the tank before entering the main shrine, believing that the water will cleanse them of their sins and impurities. The tank's serene atmosphere and the surrounding colonnade, adorned with murals depicting scenes from Hindu mythology, create a tranquil ambiance.

The main shrine of the Meenakshi Amman Temple houses the idol of Goddess Meenakshi, a resplendent figure adorned with jewels and flowers. The goddess, depicted with a parrot on her right shoulder, is a symbol of beauty, power, and compassion. Devotees offer prayers, make offerings, and seek blessings from the goddess, their hearts filled with reverence and devotion.

The shrine of Sundareswarar, the consort of Meenakshi, is located adjacent to the main shrine. The idol of Sundareswarar, a form of Lord Shiva, is depicted in a seated posture, radiating an aura of tranquility and wisdom. The shrine is a popular destination for devotees seeking blessings for marital harmony and prosperity.

The Meenakshi Amman Temple is not just a place of worship; it is a vibrant hub of cultural and religious activity. The temple hosts several festivals throughout the year, attracting a diverse array of visitors. The Chithirai Festival, celebrated in April, is the most important festival of the temple, commemorating the celestial wedding of Meenakshi and Sundareswarar. The festival features a grand procession, where the idols of the deities are carried through the streets of Madurai, accompanied by music, dance, and fanfare.

The temple's architecture, a masterpiece of Dravidian craftsmanship, is a testament to the ingenuity and creativity of its builders. The temple's gopurams, with their towering heights and intricate sculptures, are a sight to behold. The tallest gopuram, the Southern Gopuram, stands at 170 feet and is adorned with over 1,500 stucco figures.

The temple's mandapams, with their intricately carved pillars, ornate ceilings, and sprawling courtyards, are a testament to the grandeur and opulence of the Nayak dynasty, who ruled Madurai in the 16th and 17th centuries. The Nayaks were great patrons of art and architecture, and their contributions to the Meenakshi Amman Temple are evident in its magnificent structures.

The temple's sculptures, numbering in the thousands, are a visual feast for the eyes. The sculptures depict a wide range of themes, from mythological scenes to everyday life in ancient Madurai. The sculptures' intricate details, expressive faces, and graceful postures are a testament to the skill and artistry of the sculptors.

The Meenakshi Amman Temple is not just a place of worship; it is a living museum of Dravidian art and architecture. The temple's structures, sculptures, and paintings offer a glimpse into the rich cultural heritage of the region. The temple's history, spanning over two millennia, is a testament to the enduring power of faith and the human quest for spiritual enlightenment.

The temple's impact on the city of Madurai is immense. The city's economy thrives on the influx of pilgrims and tourists who come to visit the temple. The temple also plays a crucial role in the city's cultural life, with its festivals and rituals attracting a diverse array of participants.

The Meenakshi Amman Temple is not without its challenges. The temple faces issues such as overcrowding, commercialization, and pollution. However, the temple administration, along with the local community and government, is taking steps to address these issues and ensure the preservation of this iconic monument for future generations.

In conclusion, the Meenakshi Amman Temple is a cultural and architectural marvel that embodies the essence of Dravidian heritage. It is a place of worship, a center of learning, and a hub of cultural activity. The temple's grandeur, its intricate sculptures, and its rich history continue to inspire and awe visitors from all over the world.

As the city of Madurai continues to evolve, the Meenakshi Amman Temple remains a constant, a reminder of the city's glorious past and a symbol of its vibrant present. The temple's timeless appeal lies in its ability to connect people with their cultural roots, to inspire a sense of awe and wonder, and to offer a glimpse into the divine.

ᗡᗡᗡ

Madurai, a city steeped in Dravidian heritage, where the Meenakshi Amman Temple's towering gopurams pierce the sky. Explore the temple's intricate carvings and sculptures, a testament to the artistic brilliance of the region. Let the vibrant colors and intricate details of the temple complex transport you to a realm of wonder and awe.

TEN

KANCHIPURAM: CITY OF TEMPLES – A THOUSAND PILLARS OF FAITH

Kanchipuram, a city steeped in history and spirituality, is a testament to the enduring legacy of Indian civilization. Known as the "City of a Thousand Temples," Kanchipuram boasts a rich tapestry of architectural marvels, each a testament to the devotion and craftsmanship of generations past. This ancient city, located in the southern Indian state of Tamil Nadu, is a pilgrimage site of immense significance, drawing devotees and tourists alike who come to experience its unique blend of history, culture, and spirituality.

Kanchipuram's association with religion and spirituality dates back to ancient times. The city is believed to have been a major center of learning and culture during the Pallava and Chola dynasties, with numerous temples and educational institutions established during this period. Kanchipuram was also a thriving center of trade and commerce, attracting merchants and travelers from all over the world.

The city's religious landscape is dominated by its numerous temples, each with its own unique charm and architectural style. The Kailasanathar Temple, a UNESCO World Heritage Site, is one of the oldest and most significant temples in Kanchipuram. Built in the 7th century by the Pallava king Rajasimha, the temple is a masterpiece of Dravidian architecture, with its intricate carvings, soaring gopurams, and exquisite sculptures.

The temple's sanctum sanctorum houses a lingam, a representation of Lord Shiva, the Hindu god of destruction and creation. The temple's walls are adorned with sculptures depicting scenes from Hindu mythology, including the stories of Shiva, Parvati, and their children, Ganesha and Kartikeya. The Kailasanathar Temple is not just a place of worship; it is a living museum of Pallava art and architecture.

The Ekambareswarar Temple, another iconic landmark in Kanchipuram, is dedicated to Lord Shiva. The temple's main deity, Ekambareswarar, is represented by a lingam that is believed to be one of the largest in India. The temple's architecture is a blend of Dravidian and Vijayanagara styles, with towering gopurams, sprawling mandapams (pillared halls), and ornate sculptures.

The temple's thousand-pillared hall, a marvel of engineering and craftsmanship, is a major attraction. Each pillar is adorned with intricate carvings depicting scenes from Hindu mythology and everyday life in ancient Kanchipuram. The hall's acoustics are legendary, with the sound of a single clap reverberating through the entire space.

The Kamakshi Amman Temple, dedicated to Goddess Kamakshi, a form of Parvati, is another revered shrine in Kanchipuram. The temple's architecture is a blend of Dravidian and Vijayanagara styles, with a towering gopuram, a sprawling mandapam, and intricate sculptures. The temple's sanctum sanctorum houses a beautiful idol of Goddess Kamakshi, adorned with jewels and flowers. The goddess is revered for her power to grant wishes and bestow blessings upon her devotees.

The Varadharaja Perumal Temple, dedicated to Lord Vishnu, is one of the largest temple complexes in Kanchipuram. The temple's architecture is a blend of Dravidian and Vijayanagara styles, with towering gopurams, sprawling mandapams, and intricate sculptures. The temple's main deity, Varadharaja Perumal, is a form of Lord Vishnu, revered for his benevolence and compassion.

The temple complex houses several other shrines dedicated to various deities, including Goddess Lakshmi, the consort of Lord Vishnu, and Lord Anjaneya, the monkey god. The temple's tank, known as Anantha Saras, is believed to have healing properties and is a popular spot for ritual bathing.

Kanchipuram's temples are not just places of worship; they are living museums of art, architecture, and history. The temples' intricate sculptures, ornate pillars, and majestic gopurams are a testament to the skill and creativity of the artisans and architects who built them. The temples' walls are adorned with inscriptions that provide valuable insights into the history and culture of the region.

The city's rich cultural heritage is not limited to its temples. Kanchipuram is also known for its silk sarees, which are renowned for their exquisite craftsmanship and intricate designs. The city's silk weavers, who have been practicing their craft for centuries, are highly skilled and their sarees are prized possessions for women all over India.

Kanchipuram's culinary scene is another aspect of its rich cultural heritage. The city is famous for its traditional vegetarian cuisine, which is known for its unique flavors and use of fresh, locally sourced ingredients. The city's sweet shops are a haven for those with a sweet tooth, offering a wide array of delectable sweets and savories.

In conclusion, Kanchipuram is a city that seamlessly blends history, culture, and spirituality. Its numerous temples, each a testament to the devotion and craftsmanship of generations past, are a treasure trove of art, architecture, and history. The city's vibrant cultural scene, its exquisite silk sarees, and its delectable cuisine add to its allure, making it a must-visit destination for anyone seeking to experience the rich tapestry of Indian heritage.

Kanchipuram, the city of a thousand temples, a testament to the enduring power of faith and devotion. Wander through the ancient streets, each corner revealing a new temple, each with its own unique charm and history. Immerse yourself in the rich tapestry of religious and cultural traditions that have shaped this city.

ELEVEN

UJJAIN: MAHAKALESHWAR JYOTIRLINGA - ABODE OF LORD SHIVA

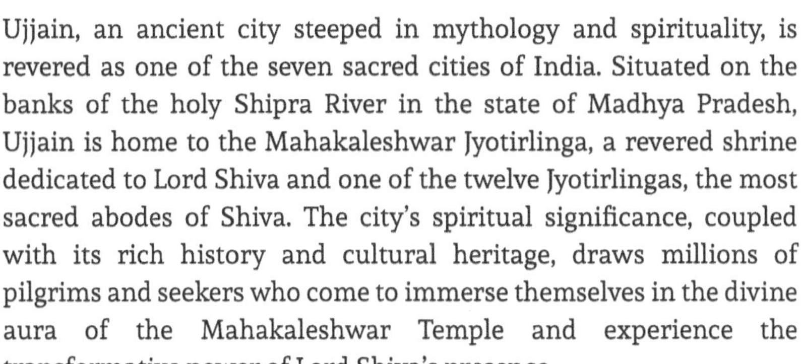

Ujjain, an ancient city steeped in mythology and spirituality, is revered as one of the seven sacred cities of India. Situated on the banks of the holy Shipra River in the state of Madhya Pradesh, Ujjain is home to the Mahakaleshwar Jyotirlinga, a revered shrine dedicated to Lord Shiva and one of the twelve Jyotirlingas, the most sacred abodes of Shiva. The city's spiritual significance, coupled with its rich history and cultural heritage, draws millions of pilgrims and seekers who come to immerse themselves in the divine aura of the Mahakaleshwar Temple and experience the transformative power of Lord Shiva's presence.

The Mahakaleshwar Temple, with its majestic architecture and serene ambiance, stands as a testament to the enduring devotion and reverence that has been showered upon Lord Shiva for centuries. The temple complex, a sprawling labyrinth of shrines, mandapams (pillared halls), and courtyards, exudes an aura of spirituality that instantly transports visitors to a realm of divine grace.

The sanctum sanctorum of the Mahakaleshwar Temple houses the Jyotirlinga, a representation of Lord Shiva as a pillar of light. The Jyotirlinga is believed to be swayambhu, meaning self-manifested, and is said to radiate immense divine energy. The lingam is adorned with a silver mask depicting the five faces of Shiva, known as the Panchamukhi Mahadev.

The temple's architecture is a harmonious blend of various styles, reflecting the diverse cultural influences that have shaped the city over centuries. The main shikhara, or tower, rises majestically towards the heavens, its intricate carvings and sculptures depicting scenes from Hindu mythology and the life of Lord Shiva. The temple's mandapams, with their ornate pillars and expansive halls, provide a space for devotees to gather, offer prayers, and participate in rituals.

The Mahakaleshwar Temple is not merely a place of worship; it is a living testament to the rich cultural and spiritual heritage of Ujjain. The temple's walls are adorned with murals and sculptures depicting scenes from the Puranas, ancient Hindu scriptures that narrate the stories of gods and goddesses. The temple also houses a museum that showcases artifacts and exhibits related to the history and mythology of Ujjain.

The Bhasma Aarti, a unique ritual performed at the Mahakaleshwar Temple, is a major draw for pilgrims and tourists alike. The aarti, performed in the early hours of the morning, involves the application of sacred ash, or bhasma, to the lingam, accompanied by the chanting of mantras and the rhythmic beat of drums. The

Bhasma Aarti is a mesmerizing spectacle that leaves a lasting impression on all who witness it.

Beyond the Mahakaleshwar Temple, Ujjain offers a wealth of spiritual experiences for the seeker. The Kal Bhairav Temple, dedicated to Kal Bhairav, a fierce manifestation of Lord Shiva, is a popular pilgrimage site. The temple is believed to be one of the eight Bhairav temples established by the goddess Parvati.

The Harsiddhi Temple, dedicated to Goddess Annapurna, the goddess of food and nourishment, is another revered shrine in Ujjain. The temple is believed to have been established by the legendary king Vikramaditya, who is said to have ruled Ujjain in the 1st century BCE.

The Gopal Mandir, dedicated to Lord Krishna, is a magnificent temple adorned with intricate carvings and sculptures. The temple's architecture is a blend of Maratha and Rajput styles, showcasing the rich cultural diversity of the region.

The Kumbh Mela, a grand religious festival held every twelve years in Ujjain, is a testament to the city's spiritual significance. Millions of pilgrims from all over the world converge on Ujjain during this auspicious occasion to take a holy dip in the Shipra River and seek blessings from the divine. The Kumbh Mela is a vibrant spectacle, with its vast crowds, colorful processions, and diverse religious and cultural events.

Ujjain's spiritual landscape is not limited to temples and shrines. The city's vibrant markets are filled with shops selling religious paraphernalia, traditional handicrafts, and local delicacies. The aroma of incense and spices fills the air, creating a sensory experience that is both invigorating and calming.

The Simhastha Kumbh Mela, held once every twelve years,

transforms Ujjain into a hub of spiritual activity. Millions of devotees gather on the banks of the Shipra River to take a holy dip, participate in religious rituals, and listen to discourses by spiritual leaders. The Kumbh Mela is a time for spiritual renewal and introspection, where the individual connects with the divine and seeks blessings for a better life.

The Ujjain Kumbh Mela is not only a religious gathering; it is also a cultural extravaganza. The mela features various cultural programs, including music and dance performances, exhibitions, and seminars. It is a platform for artists and artisans from all over India to showcase their talent and creativity.

In addition to its spiritual and cultural significance, Ujjain is also known for its historical and astronomical importance. The city was once home to the renowned astronomer and mathematician, Varahamihira, who lived in the 6th century CE. Ujjain was also the site of the Tropic of Cancer, making it a significant center for astronomical observations.

The ancient observatory, Jantar Mantar, built by Maharaja Jai Singh II of Jaipur in the 18th century, is a testament to Ujjain's astronomical heritage. The observatory houses several astronomical instruments that were used for observing celestial bodies and calculating time.

In conclusion, Ujjain is a city that seamlessly blends history, culture, and spirituality. Its ancient temples, vibrant festivals, and rich cultural heritage make it a must-visit destination for anyone seeking to experience the essence of India's spiritual heartland. The Mahakaleshwar Jyotirlinga, with its divine aura and transformative power, continues to attract millions of devotees who come to seek the blessings of Lord Shiva and embark on a journey towards spiritual enlightenment.

ᡒᡒᡒ

Ujjain, where the Mahakaleshwar Jyotirlinga, a sacred abode of Lord Shiva, radiates divine energy. Witness the mesmerizing Bhasma Aarti, a ritual that awakens the soul and connects you with the cosmic power of the universe.

TWELVE
PUSHKAR: BRAHMA TEMPLE & SACRED LAKE - A UNIQUE PILGRIMAGE

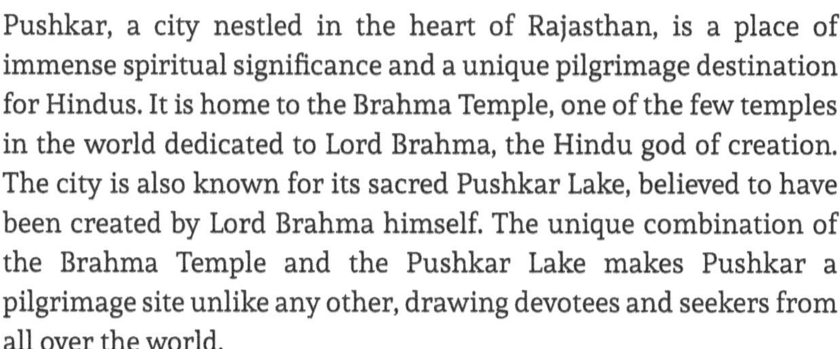

Pushkar, a city nestled in the heart of Rajasthan, is a place of immense spiritual significance and a unique pilgrimage destination for Hindus. It is home to the Brahma Temple, one of the few temples in the world dedicated to Lord Brahma, the Hindu god of creation. The city is also known for its sacred Pushkar Lake, believed to have been created by Lord Brahma himself. The unique combination of the Brahma Temple and the Pushkar Lake makes Pushkar a pilgrimage site unlike any other, drawing devotees and seekers from all over the world.

The Brahma Temple, with its distinct red spire and marble architecture, stands as a testament to the reverence and devotion that Lord Brahma commands among Hindus. The temple's sanctum sanctorum houses a life-size statue of Lord Brahma, depicted with four heads and four arms, symbolizing his omnipresence and creative power. The statue is adorned with intricate jewelry and garments, adding to its divine aura.

The temple's architecture is a blend of various styles, reflecting the diverse cultural influences that have shaped the region over centuries. The temple's walls are adorned with sculptures depicting scenes from Hindu mythology, including the story of Lord Brahma's creation of the universe. The temple also houses several smaller shrines dedicated to various deities, including Goddess Saraswati, the goddess of knowledge and learning, and Lord Vishnu, the preserver of the universe.

The Brahma Temple is not merely a place of worship; it is a living testament to the rich cultural and spiritual heritage of Pushkar. The temple hosts several festivals throughout the year, attracting a diverse array of visitors. The Kartik Purnima festival, celebrated in November, is the most important festival of the temple, commemorating the day when Lord Brahma is believed to have performed a yagna, or sacrificial ritual, at Pushkar Lake.

The festival is a grand celebration, with thousands of pilgrims taking a holy dip in the sacred lake and offering prayers at the Brahma Temple. The Pushkar Camel Fair, held annually in conjunction with the Kartik Purnima festival, is another major attraction, drawing visitors from all over the world who come to witness the spectacle of thousands of camels being traded and decorated.

The Pushkar Lake, a serene expanse of water surrounded by ghats (steps), is considered to be one of the most sacred lakes in India. According to Hindu mythology, the lake was created by Lord Brahma when a lotus flower fell from his hand. The lake is believed to have healing properties and is a popular spot for ritual bathing.

Pilgrims take a dip in the lake's holy waters, believing that it will cleanse them of their sins and grant them spiritual purification. The ghats surrounding the lake are dotted with temples and shrines dedicated to various deities, creating a serene and spiritual ambiance.

The Pushkar Lake is not just a religious site; it is also a popular tourist destination. The lake's picturesque setting, surrounded by hills and desert, attracts visitors who come to enjoy boating, photography, and simply soaking in the tranquil atmosphere. The lake is also home to a variety of migratory birds, making it a haven for birdwatchers.

The Pushkar Camel Fair, held annually on the banks of the Pushkar Lake, is a unique and vibrant event that showcases the cultural heritage of Rajasthan. The fair features a variety of activities, including camel races, camel dances, and cultural performances. It is a time for traders, farmers, and artisans from all over Rajasthan to come together and showcase their products and skills.

The Pushkar Camel Fair is not just a commercial event; it is also a cultural extravaganza. The fair features a variety of cultural programs, including music and dance performances, exhibitions, and seminars. It is a platform for artists and artisans from all over Rajasthan to showcase their talent and creativity.

Pushkar, with its unique combination of the Brahma Temple and the Pushkar Lake, is a pilgrimage site that offers a truly transformative experience. The city's spiritual ambiance, coupled with its rich cultural heritage, makes it a must-visit destination for anyone seeking to connect with the divine and explore the depths of Indian spirituality.

ppp

Pushkar, a unique pilgrimage site where the Brahma Temple and the sacred Pushkar Lake coexist in harmony. Take a dip in the holy waters, believed to have been created by Lord Brahma himself, and offer your prayers at the temple dedicated to the creator god.

THIRTEEN

DWARKA: LORD KRISHNA'S KINGDOM – ANCIENT PORT CITY OF LEGENDS

Dwarka, an ancient port city on the western coast of India, is steeped in mythology and history. It is believed to have been the dwelling place of Lord Krishna, a revered deity in Hinduism, and is considered one of the seven sacred cities of India. The city's name, derived from the Sanskrit word "dwar," meaning "door" or "gateway," and "ka," referring to Lord Brahma, the creator god, signifies its importance as a spiritual gateway.

The city's origins are shrouded in legend, with ancient texts such as the Mahabharata and the Bhagavata Purana recounting the tale of Lord Krishna's migration from Mathura to Dwarka to establish his kingdom. According to these texts, Krishna, along with his Yadava clan, built a magnificent city on the island of Kushastali, which was reclaimed from the sea. The city, known for its opulence and grandeur, was adorned with palaces, temples, and gardens.

The Dwarkadhish Temple, dedicated to Lord Krishna, is the heart and soul of Dwarka. The temple's architecture is a testament to the rich cultural heritage of the region, with its intricate carvings, soaring spires, and ornate decorations. The temple's main deity, Dwarkadhish, is a form of Lord Krishna, depicted in a standing posture, holding a flute and a conch shell. The idol is adorned with precious ornaments and garments, making it a sight to behold.

The temple complex is a labyrinth of shrines, mandapams (pillared halls), and courtyards, each with its own unique charm and significance. The Gomti Ghat, located on the banks of the Gomti River, is a sacred spot where pilgrims take a holy dip before entering the temple. The ghat is also associated with the legend of Lord Krishna, who is said to have bathed in the Gomti River every day.

The Rukmini Devi Temple, dedicated to Rukmini, the consort of Lord Krishna, is another important shrine in Dwarka. The temple's architecture is a blend of Chalukyan and Solanki styles, showcasing the diverse cultural influences that have shaped the region. The temple's sanctum sanctorum houses a beautiful idol of Rukmini, adorned with jewels and flowers. The goddess is revered for her beauty, grace, and devotion to Lord Krishna.

The Bet Dwarka, an island located off the coast of Dwarka, is believed to be the original residence of Lord Krishna. The island is home to several ancient temples, including the Bet Dwarka Temple, dedicated to Lord Krishna, and the Hanuman Dandi Temple, dedicated to Lord Hanuman, the monkey god. The island is also a popular spot for birdwatching, with a variety of migratory birds flocking to its shores during the winter months.

Dwarka's archaeological significance is immense. The city has been the subject of numerous excavations and studies, which have revealed a wealth of information about its ancient past. The excavations have unearthed remains of a well-planned city, with evidence of a sophisticated drainage system, a fort, and a harbor. The findings suggest that Dwarka was a prosperous port city with trade links to other parts of India and the world.

The Dwarka Underwater Archaeology Project, launched by the Archaeological Survey of India in 1988, has further strengthened the evidence of the city's ancient maritime heritage. The project has unearthed submerged structures, including walls, pillars, and pottery, that suggest the existence of a port city that was submerged due to a rise in sea level.

Dwarka's mythological and archaeological significance has made it a popular pilgrimage destination for centuries. Pilgrims from all over India and beyond come to Dwarka to seek the blessings of Lord Krishna and experience the divine aura that permeates the ancient city.

The city's vibrant cultural scene, with its numerous festivals and rituals, is a testament to its rich heritage. The Janmashtami festival, celebrated in honor of Lord Krishna's birth, is a major event that draws thousands of pilgrims to Dwarka. The festival is marked by colorful processions, cultural performances, and religious rituals.

The Dwarka Utsav, a cultural festival held annually, is another major attraction, showcasing the region's rich artistic traditions. The festival features music and dance performances, exhibitions, and seminars, providing a platform for artists and artisans to showcase their talent and creativity.

Dwarka's natural beauty adds to its allure. The city's pristine beaches, crystal-clear waters, and lush greenery provide a serene backdrop for spiritual contemplation and relaxation. The city is also home to a variety of marine life, making it a popular spot for snorkeling and scuba diving.

The Dwarka Lighthouse, located at the tip of the city's peninsula, offers breathtaking views of the Arabian Sea and the surrounding landscape. The lighthouse, a popular tourist attraction, is a reminder of Dwarka's maritime heritage.

In conclusion, Dwarka is a city that seamlessly blends mythology, history, and spirituality. Its ancient temples, vibrant festivals, and rich cultural heritage make it a must-visit destination for anyone seeking to experience the essence of India's spiritual heartland. The city's natural beauty, coupled with its historical and archaeological significance, makes it a unique and unforgettable destination. As the waves of the Arabian Sea continue to lap against the shores of Dwarka, the city stands tall, a beacon of hope and a symbol of India's rich and diverse cultural heritage.

ppp

*Dwarka, the ancient kingdom of Lord Krishna,
where legends come alive. Explore the Dwarkadhish
Temple, a testament to the city's rich cultural
heritage, and immerse yourself in the stories of
Krishna's divine leelas.*

FOURTEEN

MATHURA & VRINDAVAN: KRISHNA'S BIRTHPLACE & CHILDHOOD - DIVINE LOVE

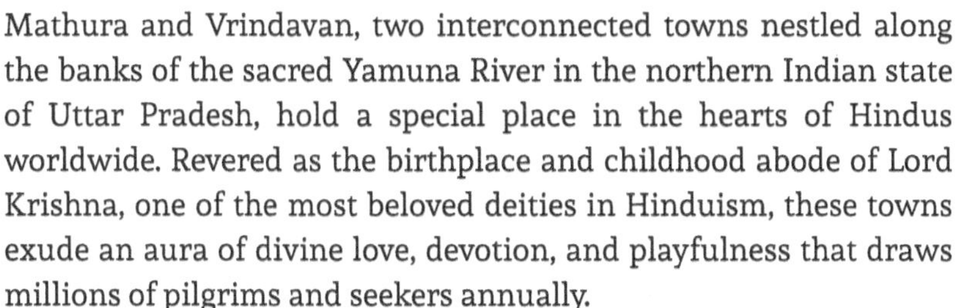

Mathura and Vrindavan, two interconnected towns nestled along the banks of the sacred Yamuna River in the northern Indian state of Uttar Pradesh, hold a special place in the hearts of Hindus worldwide. Revered as the birthplace and childhood abode of Lord Krishna, one of the most beloved deities in Hinduism, these towns exude an aura of divine love, devotion, and playfulness that draws millions of pilgrims and seekers annually.

Mathura, the birthplace of Lord Krishna, is a city steeped in history and mythology. Ancient texts such as the Mahabharata and the Bhagavata Purana narrate the tale of Krishna's miraculous birth in a prison cell to Devaki and Vasudeva, who were imprisoned by the tyrannical king Kansa. The story of Krishna's escape from Mathura as an infant and his subsequent life in Vrindavan is a tale of divine intervention, heroic deeds, and the triumph of good over evil.

The Krishna Janmabhoomi Temple, located in the heart of Mathura, is believed to be the exact site where Lord Krishna was born. The temple complex, a sprawling labyrinth of shrines, mandapams (pillared halls), and courtyards, is a testament to the enduring devotion and reverence that has been showered upon Lord Krishna for centuries.

The temple's sanctum sanctorum houses a beautiful idol of Lord Krishna as a child, depicted in a standing posture, holding a butterball in his hand. The idol is adorned with precious ornaments and garments, making it a sight to behold. Devotees offer prayers, make offerings, and seek blessings from the Lord, their hearts filled with love and devotion.

The temple complex also houses several other shrines dedicated to various deities, including Lord Vishnu, the preserver of the universe, and Goddess Lakshmi, the goddess of wealth and prosperity. The temple's architecture is a blend of various styles, reflecting the diverse cultural influences that have shaped the city over centuries.

Vrindavan, located just a few kilometers from Mathura, is where Lord Krishna spent his childhood and adolescence. The town is synonymous with Krishna's playful and mischievous nature, his love for Radha, and his divine leelas, or pastimes. Vrindavan is dotted with numerous temples, each dedicated to a different aspect of Krishna's life and his divine love for Radha.

The Banke Bihari Temple, one of the most popular shrines in Vrindavan, is dedicated to Lord Krishna in his youthful form. The temple's idol of Banke Bihari, depicted with a mischievous smile and a flute in his hand, is a sight to behold. Devotees throng to the temple to seek the blessings of the Lord, believing that his divine love can heal all wounds and bring joy and happiness into their lives.

The ISKCON Temple, also known as the Sri Krishna Balaram Mandir, is a modern temple complex dedicated to Lord Krishna and his brother Balarama. The temple, established by the International Society for Krishna Consciousness (ISKCON), is a center for spiritual learning and devotion. The temple complex houses a beautiful garden, a museum, and a restaurant that serves delicious vegetarian food.

The Prem Mandir, a relatively new temple in Vrindavan, is a magnificent structure that showcases the eternal love of Radha and Krishna. The temple's architecture is a blend of modern and traditional styles, with intricate marble carvings, colorful mosaics, and beautiful fountains. The temple's light and sound show, depicting the divine love story of Radha and Krishna, is a major attraction.

Vrindavan's spiritual landscape is not limited to temples and shrines. The town's streets are lined with ashrams and guesthouses, where pilgrims and seekers can stay and immerse themselves in the spiritual atmosphere. The town's markets are filled with shops selling religious paraphernalia, traditional clothing, and local delicacies. The aroma of incense and flowers fills the air, creating a sensory experience that is both invigorating and calming.

The Holi festival, celebrated in Vrindavan with great enthusiasm, is a major attraction. The festival, which marks the arrival of spring, is a time for revelry and celebration, with people of all ages drenching each other in colored powder and water. The Holi festival in Vrindavan is a unique experience, with the entire town transformed into a riot of colors and music.

The Rasa Lila, a traditional dance-drama depicting the divine love of Radha and Krishna, is another major attraction in Vrindavan. The dance-drama, performed by local artists, is a visual feast that showcases the rich cultural heritage of the region. The Rasa Lila is a moving and spiritually uplifting experience that leaves a lasting impression on all who witness it.

Mathura and Vrindavan, with their rich mythology, vibrant cultural scene, and spiritual significance, are destinations that offer a transformative experience for the seeker. The towns' temples, ashrams, and ghats provide a space for spiritual contemplation and introspection, while their festivals and cultural events offer a glimpse into the rich tapestry of Indian tradition.

The love of Radha and Krishna, as celebrated in these towns, is a symbol of divine love and devotion. It is a love that transcends all boundaries, a love that unites the soul with the divine. The experience of visiting Mathura and Vrindavan is not merely a pilgrimage; it is a journey of the heart, a quest for divine love and spiritual fulfillment.

ᎮᎮᎮ

Mathura and Vrindavan, the land of Krishna's birth and childhood, where divine love permeates the air. Visit the Krishna Janmabhoomi Temple and the Banke Bihari Temple, where the mischievous charm of the young Krishna captivates the hearts of devotees.

FIFTEEN

SHIRDI: SAI BABA'S SANCTUARY - A SAINT FOR ALL FAITHS

Shirdi, a small town nestled in the heart of Maharashtra, is a place of immense spiritual significance and a beacon of religious harmony. It is the home of Sai Baba, a revered saint who transcended religious boundaries and embraced people from all faiths. Sai Baba's teachings of love, compassion, and selfless service continue to inspire millions of devotees who flock to Shirdi to seek his blessings and guidance.

Sai Baba's origins are shrouded in mystery. He arrived in Shirdi as a young man, his past unknown, his identity unclear. Yet, his charismatic presence, his simple teachings, and his miraculous deeds soon attracted a devoted following. Sai Baba lived a simple life, residing in a dilapidated mosque, which he named Dwarkamai. He spent his days interacting with devotees, offering them spiritual guidance, and performing miracles that healed the sick, comforted the troubled, and uplifted the downtrodden.

Sai Baba's teachings were simple yet profound. He emphasized the importance of love, compassion, and faith in God. He taught that all religions are paths to the same divine truth and that there is no difference between Hindus and Muslims. He encouraged his devotees to lead a simple and virtuous life, to help the needy, and to always remember God.

Sai Baba's miracles were legendary. He is said to have cured the sick, turned water into oil, and even appeared in multiple places at the same time. His miracles were not just displays of supernatural power, but acts of compassion aimed at helping those in need. Sai Baba's miracles drew people from all walks of life to Shirdi, and his fame spread far and wide.

Sai Baba's Samadhi Mandir, built on the site of his final resting place, is the heart and soul of Shirdi. The temple complex, a sprawling structure of white marble, is a testament to the devotion and reverence that Sai Baba commands among his devotees. The temple's sanctum sanctorum houses the samadhi of Sai Baba, a marble tomb where his mortal remains are enshrined.

Devotees from all over the world come to Shirdi to pay homage to Sai Baba and seek his blessings. They offer prayers, light lamps, and sing bhajans (devotional songs) in his honor. The temple complex is a bustling hub of activity, with devotees from all walks of life coming together to share their faith and devotion.

The Dwarkamai Mosque, where Sai Baba lived and meditated, is another important pilgrimage site in Shirdi. The mosque, a simple structure with a tiled roof and a spacious courtyard, is a place of great spiritual significance. Devotees come to the mosque to meditate, pray, and seek the blessings of Sai Baba. The mosque is also home to the Dhuni, a sacred fire that Sai Baba lit and kept burning throughout his lifetime. The Dhuni is believed to possess healing properties and is revered by devotees.

The Chavadi, a small building that served as Sai Baba's resting place on alternate nights, is another popular pilgrimage site in Shirdi. The Chavadi is a simple structure with a wooden platform where Sai Baba used to sleep. Devotees come to the Chavadi to offer prayers and seek the blessings of Sai Baba.

The Lendi Baug, a garden located near the Samadhi Mandir, is a tranquil oasis of greenery and serenity. The garden is home to a variety of trees and plants, and is a popular spot for meditation and relaxation. The Lendi Baug also houses the Gurusthan, a neem tree under which Sai Baba is believed to have first appeared in Shirdi.

The Dixit Wada Museum, located near the Samadhi Mandir, houses a collection of artifacts and memorabilia related to Sai Baba. The museum's exhibits include Sai Baba's personal belongings, photographs, and paintings. The museum is a treasure trove of information about Sai Baba's life and teachings, and is a must-visit for all devotees.

Shirdi's spiritual significance is not limited to its temples and shrines. The town's narrow lanes, bustling markets, and vibrant cultural scene add to its charm. The town's cuisine is also heavily influenced by Sai Baba's teachings, with many restaurants and eateries offering simple yet delicious vegetarian food.

The Shirdi Sai Baba Temple Trust, established in 1922, is responsible for the management and upkeep of the temple complex and other facilities in Shirdi. The trust runs several charitable initiatives, including hospitals, schools, and orphanages, providing much-needed support to the underprivileged sections of society.

The trust also organizes various religious and cultural events throughout the year, attracting devotees from all over the world.

The Shirdi Sai Baba Punyatithi, celebrated on October 15th every year, is a major event that draws millions of devotees to Shirdi. The festival is marked by special prayers, bhajans, and processions.

In conclusion, Shirdi is a place of immense spiritual significance and a beacon of religious harmony. It is a place where people from all faiths come together to seek the blessings of Sai Baba, a saint who transcended religious boundaries and embraced all humanity. The city's temples, shrines, and other landmarks are a testament to Sai Baba's enduring legacy, and his teachings of love, compassion, and selfless service continue to inspire millions around the world.

❦❦❦

Shirdi, the sanctuary of Sai Baba, a saint for all faiths. Experience the simplicity and universality of his teachings, and seek his blessings at the Samadhi Mandir, a place of profound devotion and reverence.

SIXTEEN

SABARIMALA: LORD AYYAPPA'S FOREST ABODE - A CHALLENGING TREK

Sabarimala, nestled in the dense forests of the Western Ghats in the southern Indian state of Kerala, is a pilgrimage site of immense spiritual significance and a testament to the unwavering devotion of millions of devotees. The Sabarimala Temple, dedicated to Lord Ayyappa, a celibate deity, is a unique shrine that attracts pilgrims from all walks of life, who embark on a challenging trek through the rugged terrain to seek the blessings of the Lord and experience the divine aura that permeates this sacred abode.

The pilgrimage to Sabarimala, known as the Sabarimala Yatra, is a rigorous and demanding journey that tests the physical and mental endurance of the devotees. The trek, which covers a distance of approximately 40 kilometers, involves traversing steep hills, dense forests, and treacherous paths. Pilgrims, clad in black or saffron attire, carry the Irumudikettu, a sacred bundle containing offerings for the Lord, on their heads as they embark on this arduous journey.

The Sabarimala Yatra is not just a physical trek; it is a spiritual odyssey that involves rigorous adherence to certain customs and rituals. Pilgrims observe a 41-day period of penance, known as Vratham, before embarking on the pilgrimage. During this period, they abstain from meat, alcohol, and other worldly pleasures, and follow a strict regimen of prayers, fasting, and celibacy.

The trek to Sabarimala is a journey of self-discovery and surrender. Pilgrims, braving the harsh terrain and challenging conditions, push their limits and test their resilience. The journey is a metaphor for life, with its ups and downs, its challenges and rewards. The physical exertion of the trek, coupled with the spiritual practices, purifies the mind and body, preparing the pilgrim for a deeper connection with the divine.

The Sabarimala Temple, located atop the Sabarimala hill, is a simple yet majestic structure that exudes an aura of serenity and devotion. The temple's sanctum sanctorum houses the idol of Lord Ayyappa, a deity revered for his celibacy, courage, and compassion. The idol, believed to be self-manifested, is adorned with precious ornaments and garments, and is a sight to behold.

Devotees, after completing the arduous trek, queue up for hours to have a darshan, or glimpse, of the Lord. The darshan is a brief but intensely spiritual experience, where the devotee feels a deep connection with the divine. The temple complex also houses several other shrines dedicated to various deities, including Vavar, a Muslim saint who is believed to have been a friend of Lord Ayyappa.

The Pathinettampadi, or the eighteen holy steps, leading to the main shrine, are a significant feature of the Sabarimala Temple. Pilgrims climb these steps with great reverence, chanting prayers and seeking the blessings of the Lord. The steps are believed to symbolize the eighteen puranas, or ancient Hindu scriptures.

The Makaravilakku, a celestial light that appears on the Makar Sankranti day, is a major highlight of the Sabarimala pilgrimage. The light, which is believed to be a divine manifestation, is witnessed by thousands of devotees who gather on the hilltop to witness this celestial spectacle. The Makaravilakku is a symbol of hope and renewal, signifying the triumph of good over evil.

The Sabarimala Temple, with its unique customs, rituals, and spiritual significance, is a microcosm of India's diverse religious and cultural traditions. The temple welcomes devotees from all walks of life, irrespective of their caste, creed, or social status. The pilgrimage is a symbol of unity and brotherhood, where people from different backgrounds come together to share their faith and devotion.

The Sabarimala Temple's management, the Travancore Devaswom Board (TDB), plays a crucial role in ensuring a smooth and safe pilgrimage experience for the devotees. The TDB manages the temple's day-to-day operations, provides accommodation and food for the pilgrims, and maintains the trekking paths. The TDB also runs several charitable initiatives, including hospitals, schools, and orphanages, providing much-needed support to the underprivileged sections of society.

The Sabarimala pilgrimage, with its challenges and rewards, is a transformative experience that leaves a lasting impression on the devotees. The journey, both physical and spiritual, is a test of one's faith, endurance, and devotion. The experience of standing before the Lord Ayyappa, after days of arduous trekking and rigorous penance, is a moment of profound spiritual awakening, a moment that reaffirms one's faith and strengthens one's resolve to lead a righteous life.

❧❧❧

Sabarimala, where the arduous trek to the hilltop shrine of Lord Ayyappa is a testament to the unwavering faith of millions of devotees. Embark on this spiritual journey, embrace the challenges, and let the divine energy of Lord Ayyappa guide your path.

SEVENTEEN

KEDARNATH: HIMALAYAN SHRINE OF LORD SHIVA - A SACRED JOURNEY

Kedarnath, nestled amidst the majestic peaks of the Garhwal Himalayas in the northern Indian state of Uttarakhand, is a place of profound spiritual significance and a testament to the unwavering devotion of millions of pilgrims. Revered as one of the Char Dham, the four sacred pilgrimage sites in Hinduism, Kedarnath is home to the Kedarnath Temple, a shrine dedicated to Lord Shiva, the Hindu god of destruction and creation. The journey to Kedarnath, a challenging trek through rugged terrain, is an arduous yet spiritually rewarding experience that attracts devotees from all walks of life.

The Kedarnath Temple, situated at an altitude of 3,583 meters (11,755 feet), is surrounded by snow-capped peaks and pristine glaciers. The temple's architecture, a blend of ancient and medieval styles, reflects the rich cultural heritage of the region. The temple's sanctum sanctorum houses a conical rock formation, believed to be a manifestation of Lord Shiva, which is worshipped as the Kedarnath Jyotirlinga, one of the twelve Jyotirlingas, the most sacred abodes of Shiva.

The temple's history is steeped in mythology and legend. According to Hindu mythology, the Pandavas, the heroes of the epic Mahabharata, sought the blessings of Lord Shiva at Kedarnath to atone for their sins after the Kurukshetra war. The temple is also associated with Adi Shankaracharya, a revered philosopher and saint who is believed to have established the temple in the 8th century CE.

The Kedarnath Yatra, the pilgrimage to Kedarnath, is a journey of faith, devotion, and self-discovery. Pilgrims, clad in saffron or white attire, embark on a trek that is both physically demanding and spiritually uplifting. The trek, which covers a distance of approximately 18 kilometers (11 miles), starts from Gaurikund, a small town situated at the base of the Kedarnath peak.

The trek, which takes approximately 6-7 hours to complete, involves ascending steep slopes, crossing gushing rivers, and navigating through dense forests. The rugged terrain and the high altitude pose a challenge to the pilgrims, testing their physical and mental endurance. However, the breathtaking scenery, the crisp mountain air, and the spiritual aura that permeates the entire region make the trek a truly unforgettable experience.

The Kedarnath Yatra is not just a physical journey; it is a spiritual odyssey that involves rigorous adherence to certain customs and rituals. Pilgrims, before embarking on the trek, take a dip in the holy waters of the Gaurikund, a natural hot spring believed to possess healing properties. They also offer prayers at the Gauri Temple, dedicated to Goddess Parvati, the consort of Lord Shiva.

The trek to Kedarnath is punctuated by several stopovers, each with its own significance. Rambara, a small hamlet located halfway through the trek, is a popular resting spot for pilgrims. The hamlet offers breathtaking views of the surrounding mountains and is home to a small temple dedicated to Lord Ganesha, the remover of obstacles.

The final leg of the trek, from Rambara to Kedarnath, is the most challenging. The path becomes steeper and narrower, with the air becoming thinner as the altitude increases. However, the sight of the Kedarnath Temple, perched majestically atop the hill, fills the pilgrims with a renewed sense of energy and determination.

Upon reaching the temple, pilgrims offer prayers to Lord Shiva and seek his blessings. The temple's sanctum sanctorum is a place of profound reverence, where devotees feel a deep connection with the divine. The temple also houses several other shrines dedicated to various deities, including Goddess Parvati, Lord Ganesha, and Lord Hanuman.

The Kedarnath Yatra is not just a religious pilgrimage; it is also a cultural and social event. Pilgrims from all over India and beyond come together, transcending linguistic, regional, and social barriers. The yatra is a testament to the unifying power of faith and the human quest for spiritual enlightenment.

The Kedarnath Temple, with its rich history, magnificent architecture, and spiritual significance, is a beacon of hope and inspiration for millions of people. The temple's serene ambiance, coupled with the breathtaking natural beauty of the surrounding Himalayas, creates an atmosphere of tranquility and devotion that is truly unparalleled.

In conclusion, the Kedarnath Yatra is a journey of a lifetime, an experience that leaves an indelible mark on the hearts and minds of all who undertake it. The trek, though challenging, is a test of one's faith, endurance, and devotion. The experience of reaching the Kedarnath Temple, standing before the Jyotirlinga, and feeling the divine presence, is a moment of profound spiritual awakening, a moment that reaffirms one's faith and strengthens one's resolve to lead a righteous life.

ৡৡৡ

Kedarnath, where the Himalayan shrine of Lord Shiva awaits, nestled amidst snow-capped peaks. The challenging trek to this sacred abode is a test of devotion and endurance, but the reward is a profound spiritual experience and a connection with the divine.

EIGHTEEN

BADRINATH: VISHNU'S ABODE IN THE HIMALAYAS – CHAR DHAM PILGRIMAGE

Badrinath, nestled amidst the majestic peaks of the Garhwal Himalayas in the northern Indian state of Uttarakhand, is a place of immense spiritual significance and a beacon of devotion for millions of Hindus. Revered as one of the Char Dham, the four sacred pilgrimage sites in Hinduism, Badrinath is home to the Badrinath Temple, a shrine dedicated to Lord Vishnu, the preserver of the universe. The journey to Badrinath, a challenging trek through rugged terrain, is an arduous yet spiritually rewarding experience that attracts devotees from all walks of life, who seek the blessings of the Lord and the purification of their souls.

The Badrinath Temple, situated at an altitude of 3,133 meters (10,279 feet) on the banks of the Alaknanda River, is a magnificent structure that exudes an aura of serenity and devotion. The temple's architecture, a blend of ancient and medieval styles, reflects the rich cultural heritage of the region. The temple's main deity, Badrinarayan, is a form of Lord Vishnu, depicted in a meditative posture, with his consort, Lakshmi, seated beside him.

The temple's history is steeped in mythology and legend. According to Hindu mythology, Lord Vishnu meditated in Badrinath for thousands of years, protected by his consort, Lakshmi, who took the form of a Badri tree (Indian Jujube) to shield him from the harsh weather conditions. The temple is also associated with Adi Shankaracharya, a revered philosopher and saint who is believed to have established the temple in the 8th century CE.

The Badrinath Yatra, the pilgrimage to Badrinath, is a journey of faith, devotion, and self-discovery. Pilgrims, clad in saffron or white attire, embark on a trek that is both physically demanding and spiritually uplifting. The trek, which covers a distance of approximately 24 kilometers (15 miles), starts from Joshimath, a town situated at the base of the Nilkantha peak.

The trek, which takes approximately 8-9 hours to complete, involves ascending steep slopes, crossing gushing rivers, and navigating through dense forests. The rugged terrain and the high altitude pose a challenge to the pilgrims, testing their physical and mental endurance. However, the breathtaking scenery, the crisp mountain air, and the spiritual aura that permeates the entire region make the trek a truly unforgettable experience.

The Badrinath Yatra is not just a physical journey; it is a spiritual odyssey that involves rigorous adherence to certain customs and rituals. Pilgrims, before embarking on the trek, take a dip in the holy waters of the Tapt Kund, a natural hot spring believed to possess healing properties. They also offer prayers at the Narasimha Temple, dedicated to Lord Narasimha, a fierce avatar of Lord

Vishnu.

The trek to Badrinath is punctuated by several stopovers, each with its own significance. Mana, the last village before the temple, is believed to be the gateway to heaven. The village is home to several ancient temples and caves, including the Vyas Gufa, where the sage Veda Vyasa is said to have composed the Mahabharata.

The final leg of the trek, from Mana to Badrinath, is the most challenging. The path becomes steeper and narrower, with the air becoming thinner as the altitude increases. However, the sight of the Badrinath Temple, nestled amidst the majestic peaks of the Himalayas, fills the pilgrims with a renewed sense of energy and determination.

Upon reaching the temple, pilgrims offer prayers to Lord Badrinarayan and seek his blessings. The temple's sanctum sanctorum is a place of profound reverence, where devotees feel a deep connection with the divine. The temple also houses several other shrines dedicated to various deities, including Goddess Lakshmi, Lord Ganesha, and Lord Hanuman.

The Badrinath Yatra is not just a religious pilgrimage; it is also a cultural and social event. Pilgrims from all over India and beyond come together, transcending linguistic, regional, and social barriers. The yatra is a testament to the unifying power of faith and the human quest for spiritual enlightenment.

The Badrinath Temple, with its rich history, magnificent architecture, and spiritual significance, is a beacon of hope and inspiration for millions of people. The temple's serene ambiance, coupled with the breathtaking natural beauty of the surrounding Himalayas, creates an atmosphere of tranquility and devotion that is truly unparalleled.

In conclusion, the Badrinath Yatra is a journey of a lifetime, an experience that leaves an indelible mark on the hearts and minds of all who undertake it. The trek, though challenging, is a test of one's faith, endurance, and devotion. The experience of reaching the Badrinath Temple, standing before the Badrinarayan deity, and feeling the divine presence, is a moment of profound spiritual awakening, a moment that reaffirms one's faith and strengthens one's resolve to lead a righteous life.

ᐅᐅᐅ

Badrinath, another Himalayan gem, where Lord Vishnu's abode offers solace and blessings. The Badrinath Yatra, a pilgrimage that tests one's physical and spiritual limits, leads to a profound connection with the divine and a deeper understanding of oneself.

NINETEEN

HEMKUND SAHIB: SIKH GURUDWARA AT HIGH ALTITUDE – SPIRITUAL SERENITY

Hemkund Sahib, a revered Sikh pilgrimage site nestled amidst the breathtaking Himalayas in the northern Indian state of Uttarakhand, is a testament to the unwavering devotion and spiritual fortitude of the Sikh community. Situated at an altitude of 4,632 meters (15,200 feet) above sea level, Hemkund Sahib is one of the highest altitude Gurudwaras (Sikh temples) in the world, and its pristine beauty and serene ambiance offer a unique spiritual experience for all who embark on the arduous journey to this sacred site.

The journey to Hemkund Sahib is an adventure in itself, a pilgrimage that tests the physical and mental endurance of the devotees. The trek, which covers a distance of approximately 19 kilometers (12 miles), starts from Govindghat, a small town situated at the base of the Hemkund Sahib peak. The trek, which takes approximately two days to complete, involves ascending steep slopes, crossing gushing rivers, and navigating through dense forests. The rugged terrain and the high altitude pose a challenge to the pilgrims, but the breathtaking scenery, the crisp mountain air, and the spiritual aura that permeates the entire region make the trek a truly unforgettable experience.

The Hemkund Sahib Gurudwara, perched on the banks of the pristine Hemkund Lake, is a sight to behold. The Gurudwara, a simple yet elegant structure made of white marble, is a symbol of Sikh devotion and resilience. The Gurudwara's sanctum sanctorum houses the Guru Granth Sahib, the holy scripture of the Sikhs, which is revered as the eternal Guru. Devotees offer prayers, sing hymns, and seek blessings from the Guru Granth Sahib, their hearts filled with gratitude and reverence.

The Hemkund Lake, a glacial lake surrounded by snow-capped peaks, is considered to be sacred by the Sikhs. According to Sikh tradition, Guru Gobind Singh, the tenth Sikh Guru, meditated on the banks of this lake in a previous life. The lake's crystal-clear waters, reflecting the surrounding mountains and the blue sky, create a mesmerizing spectacle that fills the heart with peace and tranquility.

The Hemkund Sahib Gurudwara is not just a place of worship; it is a symbol of interfaith harmony and tolerance. The Gurudwara welcomes people from all faiths and backgrounds, offering them a place to meditate, pray, and connect with the divine. The langar, or community kitchen, is a testament to the Sikh principle of seva, or selfless service, where volunteers prepare and serve free meals to thousands of pilgrims every day, regardless of their caste, creed, or social status.

The Hemkund Sahib Yatra, the pilgrimage to Hemkund Sahib, is a time of great spiritual fervor and celebration. The yatra season, which usually lasts from May to October, sees thousands of pilgrims from all over the world converge on this sacred site. The yatra is a time for introspection, self-discovery, and spiritual renewal. The pilgrims, braving the challenges of the trek and the harsh weather conditions, are rewarded with a sense of peace, tranquility, and a deeper connection with the divine.

The Hemkund Sahib Gurudwara, with its pristine beauty, serene ambiance, and spiritual significance, is a beacon of hope and inspiration for millions of people. The Gurudwara's message of faith, devotion, and selfless service resonates with people from all walks of life, making it a truly universal place of worship.

The Gurudwara's management, the Hemkund Sahib Management Trust (HSMT), plays a crucial role in ensuring a smooth and safe pilgrimage experience for the devotees. The HSMT manages the Gurudwara's day-to-day operations, provides accommodation and food for the pilgrims, and maintains the trekking paths. The HSMT also runs several charitable initiatives, including medical camps and environmental conservation projects.

The Hemkund Sahib Yatra, though physically demanding, is a journey of a lifetime, an experience that leaves an indelible mark on the hearts and minds of all who undertake it. The trek, the darshan of the Guru Granth Sahib, the dip in the holy Hemkund Lake, and the experience of sharing langar with fellow pilgrims, are all moments of profound spiritual significance that leave a lasting impact on the soul.

Hemkund Sahib, a high-altitude Sikh Gurudwara that embodies the spirit of devotion and resilience. Embark on the arduous trek to this sacred site and experience the tranquility and spiritual serenity that emanate from its pristine surroundings.

TWENTY

VAISHNO DEVI: MOUNTAIN SHRINE OF THE GODDESS - A TEST OF DEVOTION

Vaishno Devi, nestled amidst the majestic Trikuta Mountains in the northern Indian state of Jammu and Kashmir, is a revered pilgrimage site that draws millions of devotees every year. This sacred shrine, dedicated to the goddess Vaishno Devi, is believed to be a manifestation of the divine feminine energy, Shakti. The arduous journey to the shrine, a 13-kilometer trek through challenging terrain, is a test of devotion and endurance, and a testament to the unwavering faith of the pilgrims who embark on this spiritual quest.

The Vaishno Devi Yatra, the pilgrimage to the shrine, is a transformative experience that involves both physical exertion and spiritual contemplation. Pilgrims, clad in saffron or white attire, begin their journey from the base camp of Katra, a bustling town nestled in the foothills of the Trikuta Mountains. The trek, which takes approximately 6-8 hours to complete, is a winding path that ascends through scenic landscapes, dense forests, and rocky terrains.

The journey is arduous, with steep climbs and narrow passages, testing the physical endurance of the pilgrims. However, the breathtaking views of the surrounding mountains, the soothing sounds of nature, and the spiritual ambiance that permeates the entire region make the trek a truly unforgettable experience. The pilgrims, chanting hymns and prayers, draw strength and inspiration from their faith, pushing their limits to reach the holy shrine.

The Vaishno Devi Yatra is not just a physical journey; it is a spiritual odyssey that involves rigorous adherence to certain customs and rituals. Pilgrims, before embarking on the trek, take a dip in the holy Banganga River, a ritual that is believed to cleanse the body and soul. They also offer prayers at the Bhairon Temple, dedicated to Bhairon Nath, a fierce manifestation of Lord Shiva, who is believed to be the guardian of the Vaishno Devi shrine.

The trek to the shrine is punctuated by several stopovers, each with its unique significance. The Ardhkuwari Cave, located halfway through the trek, is a sacred site where the goddess Vaishno Devi is believed to have meditated for nine months. The cave is a narrow passage that can only be accessed by crawling, symbolizing the need for humility and surrender in the pursuit of spiritual enlightenment.

The Bhawan, the main shrine of Vaishno Devi, is located at the end of the arduous trek. The shrine, a cave-like structure, houses the three natural rock formations, known as the Pindis, which are worshipped as the manifestations of the goddess Vaishno Devi. The Pindis, representing the three forms of Shakti - Maha Kali, Maha Lakshmi, and Maha Saraswati, are believed to be self-manifested and are revered for their divine power and blessings.

The darshan of the Pindis is a deeply spiritual experience, where devotees feel a profound connection with the divine feminine energy. The shrine's tranquil ambiance, coupled with the chanting of hymns and the aroma of incense, creates an atmosphere of reverence and devotion that is truly unparalleled.

The Vaishno Devi Yatra is not just a religious pilgrimage; it is also a cultural and social event. Pilgrims from all over India and beyond come together, transcending linguistic, regional, and social barriers. The yatra is a testament to the unifying power of faith and the human quest for spiritual enlightenment.

The Vaishno Devi Shrine Board, the governing body of the shrine, plays a crucial role in ensuring a smooth and safe pilgrimage experience for the devotees. The board manages the shrine's day-to-day operations, provides accommodation and food for the pilgrims, and maintains the trekking paths. The board also runs several charitable initiatives, including hospitals, schools, and orphanages, providing much-needed support to the underprivileged sections of society.

The Vaishno Devi Yatra, with its challenges and rewards, is a transformative experience that leaves a lasting impression on the devotees. The journey, both physical and spiritual, is a test of one's faith, endurance, and devotion. The experience of reaching the Bhawan, standing before the Pindis, and feeling the divine presence, is a moment of profound spiritual awakening, a moment that reaffirms one's faith and strengthens one's resolve to lead a righteous life.

ॐॐॐ

Vaishno Devi, a mountain shrine where the goddess Vaishno Devi's energy manifests in three Pindis. The challenging trek to this sacred abode is a test of devotion and a journey of self-discovery, leading to a profound connection with the divine feminine energy.

TWENTY-ONE
AMARNATH: ICE LINGAM CAVE SHRINE - A MYSTICAL PILGRIMAGE

Amarnath, nestled high in the Himalayas in the northern Indian state of Jammu and Kashmir, is a site of profound spiritual significance and a testament to the enduring power of faith and devotion. The Amarnath Yatra, the annual pilgrimage to the Amarnath Cave, is a challenging yet spiritually rewarding journey that draws thousands of pilgrims from all walks of life, who seek the blessings of Lord Shiva and the purification of their souls.

The Amarnath Cave, located at an altitude of 3,888 meters (12,760 feet), is a natural wonder that houses an ice stalagmite, believed to be a manifestation of Lord Shiva, known as the Amarnath Lingam. The lingam, formed naturally from the freezing of dripping water, waxes and wanes with the lunar cycle, reaching its full size during the summer months when the pilgrimage takes place. This unique natural phenomenon, coupled with the cave's breathtaking setting amidst snow-capped peaks and glaciers, makes the Amarnath Yatra a truly mystical and awe-inspiring experience.

The Amarnath Yatra, which typically takes place between June and August, is a test of faith, endurance, and devotion. Pilgrims, clad in warm clothing and carrying essentials for the arduous journey, embark on a trek that is both physically demanding and spiritually uplifting. The trek, which can be approached from two routes – the traditional Pahalgam route and the shorter Baltal route – involves traversing rugged terrain, crossing gushing rivers, and navigating through treacherous mountain passes.

The Pahalgam route, the longer of the two routes, is a 46-kilometer (29-mile) trek that takes approximately 4-5 days to complete. The trek starts from Pahalgam, a picturesque town nestled in the Lidder Valley. The route passes through scenic meadows, dense forests, and snow-clad mountains, offering breathtaking views of the surrounding landscape. Pilgrims make stopovers at various camps along the way, including Chandanwari, Sheshnag, and Panjtarni, where they rest and replenish their supplies before continuing their journey.

The Baltal route, a shorter but steeper alternative, is a 14-kilometer (9-mile) trek that can be completed in a day or two. The trek starts from Baltal, a base camp located at a higher altitude than Pahalgam. The route is more challenging than the Pahalgam route, with steep ascents and descents, but it offers spectacular views of the surrounding glaciers and snow-capped peaks.

The Amarnath Yatra is not just a physical journey; it is a spiritual odyssey that involves rigorous adherence to certain customs and rituals. Pilgrims, before embarking on the trek, take a dip in the holy Amarnath River, a ritual that is believed to cleanse the body and soul. They also offer prayers at the Amarnath Temple, a small shrine located near the cave, seeking the blessings of Lord Shiva for a safe and successful journey.

The trek to the Amarnath Cave is punctuated by several stopovers, each with its unique significance. Sheshnag, a picturesque lake located at an altitude of 3,574 meters (11,726 feet), is a popular stopover where pilgrims rest and take a dip in the lake's holy waters. The lake is named after Sheshnag, the serpent god, who is believed to reside in the lake.

Panjtarni, another important stopover, is a confluence of five rivers that are believed to have originated from the five heads of Lord Shiva. Pilgrims take a dip in the confluence, believing that it will wash away their sins and grant them spiritual purification.

The final leg of the trek, from Panjtarni to the Amarnath Cave, is the most challenging. The path becomes steeper and narrower, with the air becoming thinner as the altitude increases. However, the sight of the cave, nestled amidst snow-capped peaks, fills the pilgrims with a renewed sense of energy and determination.

Upon reaching the cave, pilgrims offer prayers to the Amarnath Lingam and seek the blessings of Lord Shiva. The cave's atmosphere is one of profound reverence and devotion, with pilgrims chanting hymns and mantras, their hearts filled with gratitude and awe. The darshan of the Amarnath Lingam is a deeply spiritual experience, believed to cleanse the soul and grant liberation from the cycle of birth and death.

The Amarnath Yatra is not just a religious pilgrimage; it is also a cultural and social event. Pilgrims from all over India and beyond come together, transcending linguistic, regional, and social barriers. The yatra is a testament to the unifying power of faith and the human quest for spiritual enlightenment.

The Shri Amarnathji Shrine Board (SASB), the governing body of the shrine, plays a crucial role in ensuring a smooth and safe pilgrimage experience for the devotees. The board manages the shrine's day-to-day operations, provides accommodation and food for the pilgrims, and maintains the trekking paths. The SASB also runs several charitable initiatives, including medical camps and environmental conservation projects.

The Amarnath Yatra, with its challenges and rewards, is a transformative experience that leaves a lasting impression on the devotees. The journey, both physical and spiritual, is a test of one's faith, endurance, and devotion. The experience of reaching the Amarnath Cave, standing before the ice lingam, and feeling the divine presence, is a moment of profound spiritual awakening, a moment that reaffirms one's faith and strengthens one's resolve to lead a righteous life.

ᛒᛒᛒ

Amarnath, where the mystical ice lingam cave shrine of Lord Shiva awaits. Embark on a pilgrimage to this sacred site, brave the challenges of the trek, and experience the divine energy that permeates the cave, believed to cleanse the soul and grant liberation.

TWENTY-TWO

GANGOTRI & YAMUNOTRI: SOURCES OF THE GANGES & YAMUNA - HOLY RIVERS

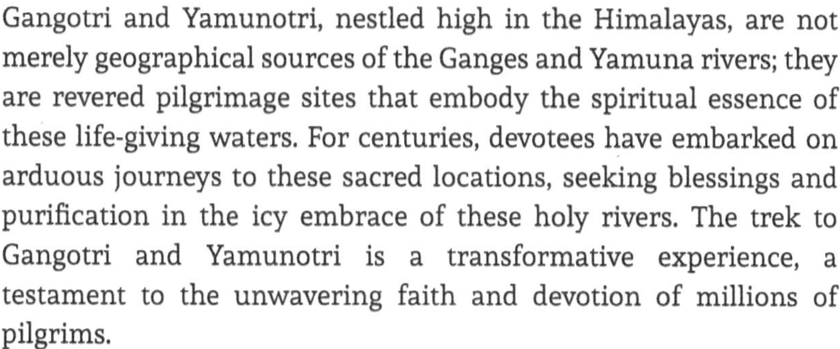

Gangotri and Yamunotri, nestled high in the Himalayas, are not merely geographical sources of the Ganges and Yamuna rivers; they are revered pilgrimage sites that embody the spiritual essence of these life-giving waters. For centuries, devotees have embarked on arduous journeys to these sacred locations, seeking blessings and purification in the icy embrace of these holy rivers. The trek to Gangotri and Yamunotri is a transformative experience, a testament to the unwavering faith and devotion of millions of pilgrims.

Gangotri, situated at an elevation of 3,100 meters (10,200 feet) above sea level, is the source of the Bhagirathi River, one of the main tributaries of the Ganges. The river emerges from the Gangotri Glacier, a vast expanse of ice and snow that feeds the Ganges and sustains life in the plains below. The Gangotri Temple, dedicated to Goddess Ganga, the personification of the Ganges River, is a simple yet majestic structure that exudes an aura of tranquility and reverence. The temple's sanctum sanctorum houses a black stone idol of Goddess Ganga, adorned with flowers and garlands. Devotees offer prayers, make offerings, and seek blessings from the goddess, their hearts filled with gratitude and awe.

The journey to Gangotri is an arduous trek that involves traversing rugged terrain, crossing gushing streams, and navigating through dense forests. The trek, which can be approached from two routes – the traditional Gangotri trek route and the shorter Harsil route – is a test of physical endurance and mental fortitude. However, the breathtaking scenery, the crisp mountain air, and the spiritual aura that permeates the entire region make the trek a truly unforgettable experience.

The Gangotri trek route, which covers a distance of approximately 18 kilometers (11 miles), starts from Uttarkashi, a town nestled in the Bhagirathi Valley. The route passes through scenic villages, lush meadows, and dense forests, offering glimpses of the snow-capped peaks of the Himalayas. Pilgrims make stopovers at various camps along the way, including Bhojbasa, a popular camping site that offers stunning views of the Gangotri Glacier.

The Harsil route, a shorter alternative, is a 7-kilometer (4-mile) trek that starts from Harsil, a picturesque village located at a higher altitude than Uttarkashi. The route is less challenging than the Gangotri trek route, but it still requires a good level of fitness and stamina. The trek passes through apple orchards, pine forests, and rhododendron groves, offering breathtaking views of the surrounding mountains.

Upon reaching Gangotri, pilgrims take a dip in the icy waters of the Bhagirathi River, a ritual that is believed to cleanse the body and soul of all sins. They also offer prayers at the Gangotri Temple, seeking the blessings of Goddess Ganga for a prosperous and fulfilling life. The temple complex is a bustling hub of activity during the pilgrimage season, with devotees from all over India and beyond thronging to the shrine.

Yamunotri, situated at an elevation of 3,293 meters (10,804 feet) above sea level, is the source of the Yamuna River, a major tributary of the Ganges. The river emerges from the Yamunotri Glacier, a massive ice formation that feeds the Yamuna and sustains life in the plains below. The Yamunotri Temple, dedicated to Goddess Yamuna, the personification of the Yamuna River, is a simple yet elegant structure that exudes an aura of tranquility and devotion. The temple's sanctum sanctorum houses a black marble idol of Goddess Yamuna, adorned with flowers and garlands. Devotees offer prayers, make offerings, and seek blessings from the goddess, their hearts filled with gratitude and awe.

The journey to Yamunotri is a challenging trek that involves traversing rugged terrain, crossing glacial streams, and navigating through dense forests. The trek, which covers a distance of approximately 13 kilometers (8 miles), starts from Janki Chatti, a small town located at the base of the Yamunotri peak. The trek, which takes approximately 6-7 hours to complete, is a test of physical endurance and mental fortitude. However, the breathtaking scenery, the crisp mountain air, and the spiritual aura that permeates the entire region make the trek a truly unforgettable experience.

Upon reaching Yamunotri, pilgrims take a dip in the icy waters of the Yamuna River, a ritual that is believed to cleanse the body and soul of all sins. They also offer prayers at the Yamunotri Temple, seeking the blessings of Goddess Yamuna for a prosperous and fulfilling life. The temple complex is a bustling hub of activity during the pilgrimage season, with devotees from all over India and beyond thronging to the shrine.

The Gangotri and Yamunotri Yatra, the pilgrimage to these sacred sites, is a journey of faith, devotion, and self-discovery. The trek, though challenging, is a test of one's endurance and a testament to the unwavering faith of the pilgrims. The experience of reaching the holy shrines, taking a dip in the icy waters, and offering prayers to the goddesses, is a moment of profound spiritual awakening, a moment that reaffirms one's faith and strengthens one's resolve to lead a righteous life.

❦❦❦

Gangotri and Yamunotri, the sources of the holy rivers Ganges and Yamuna, where pilgrims seek purification and blessings. The trek to these sacred sites is an arduous yet spiritually rewarding journey that allows one to connect with the life-giving waters and the divine energy that flows through them.

TWENTY-THREE

PURI: JAGANNATH TEMPLE - LORD OF THE UNIVERSE'S CHARIOT FESTIVAL

Puri, a coastal city in the eastern Indian state of Odisha, is synonymous with the Jagannath Temple, a revered shrine dedicated to Lord Jagannath, an incarnation of Lord Vishnu, the preserver of the universe. The temple, with its towering deula (sanctum sanctorum), intricate carvings, and vibrant festivals, is a testament to the rich cultural and spiritual heritage of the region. However, it is the annual Rath Yatra, or chariot festival, that truly sets Puri apart, drawing millions of devotees and tourists who come to witness the grand spectacle of Lord Jagannath's journey on a colossal chariot.

The Jagannath Temple, a UNESCO World Heritage Site, is an architectural marvel that dates back to the 12th century. The temple complex, a sprawling labyrinth of shrines, mandapams (pillared halls), and courtyards, exudes an aura of spirituality and grandeur that leaves visitors spellbound. The temple's main deity, Lord

Jagannath, is a unique and enigmatic figure, depicted with large round eyes and a distinctive wooden form. The deity, along with his siblings Balabhadra and Subhadra, is worshipped with great reverence and devotion by millions of Hindus.

The Rath Yatra, which takes place in the month of Ashadha (June-July), is the most important festival in Puri. The festival commemorates the annual journey of Lord Jagannath, along with his siblings, from the main temple to the Gundicha Temple, a shrine located about three kilometers away. The deities are placed on towering chariots, or raths, which are then pulled by thousands of devotees through the streets of Puri.

The raths, which are built anew every year, are massive structures made of wood and decorated with intricate carvings and colorful fabrics. The Nandighosa, the chariot of Lord Jagannath, is the tallest of the three chariots, standing at 45 feet tall and weighing over 13 tons. The Taladhwaja, the chariot of Balabhadra, is 44 feet tall and the Darpadalana, the chariot of Subhadra, is 43 feet tall.

The Rath Yatra is a spectacular sight to behold. The streets of Puri are thronged with millions of devotees, who chant hymns and prayers as they pull the chariots. The air is filled with the sound of conches, bells, and drums, creating a festive and vibrant atmosphere. The procession of the chariots, accompanied by musicians, dancers, and acrobats, is a visual feast that showcases the rich cultural traditions of Odisha.

The Rath Yatra is not just a religious festival; it is a social and cultural event that brings people from all walks of life together. The festival is a celebration of unity, diversity, and devotion. People from different castes, creeds, and religions participate in the festival, transcending social barriers and reinforcing the message of universal brotherhood.

The Rath Yatra is also a time for feasting and merrymaking. Devotees prepare and offer a variety of delicacies to Lord Jagannath, who is believed to be a connoisseur of food. The prasad, or food offered to the deity, is then distributed among the devotees, who partake in it as a sacred meal.

The Rath Yatra is a unique and vibrant festival that showcases the rich cultural heritage of Odisha. The festival's rituals, traditions, and customs are deeply rooted in Hindu mythology and have been passed down through generations. The festival is a testament to the enduring power of faith and the human quest for spiritual enlightenment.

The Jagannath Temple, with its rich history, magnificent architecture, and spiritual significance, is a beacon of hope and inspiration for millions of people. The temple's annual Rath Yatra, a grand spectacle of devotion and celebration, is a testament to the enduring power of faith and the human quest for spiritual enlightenment.

The temple's administration, the Shree Jagannath Temple Administration (SJTA), plays a crucial role in organizing and managing the Rath Yatra. The SJTA, in collaboration with the state government and various other agencies, ensures a smooth and safe pilgrimage experience for the millions of devotees who visit Puri during the festival.

The Rath Yatra, with its challenges and rewards, is a transformative experience that leaves a lasting impression on the devotees. The journey, both physical and spiritual, is a test of one's faith, endurance, and devotion. The experience of pulling the chariots, witnessing the grand procession, and partaking in the prasad, is a moment of profound spiritual awakening, a moment that reaffirms one's faith and strengthens one's resolve to lead a righteous life.

In conclusion, the Rath Yatra in Puri is not just a festival; it is a celebration of life, faith, and community. It is a time for introspection, self-discovery, and spiritual renewal. It is a time for people from all walks of life to come together and share in the joy of devotion. The Rath Yatra, with its vibrant colors, rhythmic sounds, and spiritual fervor, is a testament to the enduring power of faith and the human quest for divine connection.

Puri, where the Jagannath Temple's annual Rath Yatra, a grand spectacle of devotion and celebration, brings together millions of devotees. Witness the procession of the towering chariots and experience the vibrant colors, rhythmic sounds, and spiritual fervor that permeate this unique festival.

TWENTY-FOUR

KONARK: SUN TEMPLE - A UNESCO WORLD HERITAGE SITE OF ARCHITECTURAL BRILLIANCE

Konark, a small town on the coast of Odisha, India, is home to a marvel of ancient architecture that continues to inspire awe and wonder - the Sun Temple.A UNESCO World Heritage Site, the Konark Sun Temple is a testament to the ingenuity, skill, and devotion of the artisans and engineers who built it in the 13th century. Its unique design, intricate carvings, and symbolic representation of the sun god Surya make it an extraordinary monument that captures the essence of India's rich cultural and spiritual heritage.

The Konark Sun Temple, also known as the Black Pagoda, is a

masterpiece of Kalinga architecture, a style that flourished in the region during the medieval period. The temple, built by King Narasimhadeva I of the Eastern Ganga dynasty, is designed in the shape of a colossal chariot, complete with wheels, horses, and a charioteer. This unique architectural concept is a symbolic representation of the sun god Surya's celestial journey across the sky.

The temple's main structure, the deula, is a towering edifice that rises to a height of 229 feet. The deula is adorned with intricate carvings depicting various deities, celestial beings, and scenes from Hindu mythology. The temple's walls are covered with sculptures of elephants, horses, lions, and mythical creatures, each intricately carved with minute details. The temple's platform, or Jagati, is shaped like a chariot with twelve pairs of wheels, each representing the twelve months of the year. The wheels are intricately carved with spokes, hubs, and rims, and are adorned with figures of maidens and warriors.

The Konark Sun Temple is not just a religious monument; it is a celebration of art, architecture, and engineering. The temple's intricate carvings and sculptures are a testament to the skill and creativity of the artisans who built it. The temple's unique design, with its chariot-shaped platform and towering deula, is a marvel of engineering that continues to amaze and inspire visitors.

The temple's symbolic representation of the sun god Surya is evident in its every aspect. The twelve pairs of wheels represent the twelve months of the year, and the seven horses that pull the chariot represent the seven days of the week. The temple's main entrance, facing east, allows the first rays of the rising sun to illuminate the sanctum sanctorum, where the idol of Surya was once housed.

The Konark Sun Temple's cultural and religious significance is immense. The temple was a major center of pilgrimage and worship during the medieval period, attracting devotees from all over India. The temple's annual Chandrabhaga Mela, a festival celebrated in honor of the sun god Surya, is still a major event that draws thousands of visitors to Konark.

The temple's architectural brilliance has also earned it a place on the UNESCO World Heritage List. The temple is considered to be a masterpiece of Kalinga architecture, and its intricate carvings and sculptures are a testament to the rich cultural heritage of the region. The temple's unique design, with its chariot-shaped platform and towering deula, is a marvel of engineering that continues to amaze and inspire visitors.

The Konark Sun Temple, like many ancient monuments, has faced the ravages of time and natural calamities. The temple's main structure, the deula, has collapsed, and many of its sculptures have been damaged or lost. However, the Archaeological Survey of India has undertaken extensive restoration and conservation work to preserve this architectural gem for future generations.

The Konark Sun Temple is not just a monument of the past; it is a living testament to the enduring spirit of human creativity and devotion. The temple continues to inspire awe and wonder in all who visit it, and its legacy continues to live on in the hearts and minds of people around the world.

The Sun Temple's intricate carvings and sculptures are not just decorative elements; they are a visual representation of the rich tapestry of Hindu mythology and philosophy. The temple's walls are adorned with sculptures of various deities, including Surya, the sun god, Vishnu, the preserver, and Shiva, the destroyer. The sculptures depict scenes from the Ramayana and the Mahabharata, two of the most important epics in Hindu mythology. The temple's erotic sculptures, known as mithunas, are a testament to the celebration of life and fertility in ancient Indian culture.

The Sun Temple's architecture is not just a display of artistic skill; it is also a reflection of the scientific and astronomical knowledge of the time. The temple's twelve pairs of wheels are not just decorative elements; they are a sundial that accurately measures time. The temple's main entrance, facing east, is aligned with the rising sun, allowing the first rays of the sun to illuminate the sanctum sanctorum.

The Sun Temple's significance is not limited to its religious and cultural aspects; it is also a symbol of Odisha's rich history and heritage. The temple was built during the reign of the Eastern Ganga dynasty, which ruled over the region from the 11th to the 15th century. The Eastern Ganga dynasty was known for its patronage of art and architecture, and the Konark Sun Temple is a testament to their legacy.

The Konark Sun Temple's story is one of resilience and survival. The temple has withstood the ravages of time, natural calamities, and invasions. The temple's main structure, the deula, collapsed in the 19th century, but its ruins continue to attract visitors from all over the world. The temple's sculptures, though damaged and weathered, still retain their beauty and power, and continue to inspire awe and wonder.

The Konark Sun Temple is not just a monument of the past; it is a living testament to the enduring spirit of human creativity and devotion. The temple continues to inspire awe and wonder in all who visit it, and its legacy continues to live on in the hearts and minds of people around the world.

ppp

Konark, where the Sun Temple, a UNESCO World Heritage Site, stands as a testament to the architectural brilliance of ancient India. Explore the temple's intricate carvings and sculptures, a visual representation of Hindu mythology and philosophy, and marvel at its unique design that captures the celestial journey of the sun god Surya.

TWENTY-FIVE

CHAPTER TITLE IS OF AJMER (15), IN SUMMARY ALSO SARNATH NOT MENTIONED

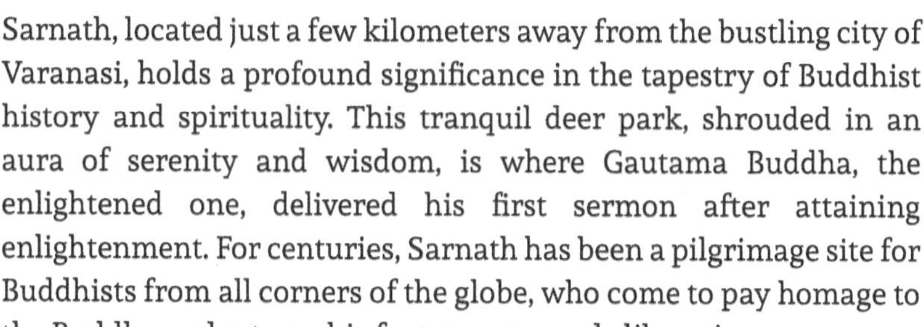

Sarnath, located just a few kilometers away from the bustling city of Varanasi, holds a profound significance in the tapestry of Buddhist history and spirituality. This tranquil deer park, shrouded in an aura of serenity and wisdom, is where Gautama Buddha, the enlightened one, delivered his first sermon after attaining enlightenment. For centuries, Sarnath has been a pilgrimage site for Buddhists from all corners of the globe, who come to pay homage to the Buddha and retrace his footsteps towards liberation.

Stepping into Sarnath is like entering a time capsule, where the echoes of ancient wisdom still resonate through the air. The Dhamek Stupa, a towering cylindrical structure, stands as a testament to the Buddha's first sermon, known as the

Dharmachakra Pravartana or "Turning of the Wheel of Dharma." This momentous event marked the beginning of the Buddha's teachings and the spread of Buddhism throughout the world.

The Dhamek Stupa, built in the 5th century CE by Emperor Ashoka, a great patron of Buddhism, is a magnificent structure that dominates the Sarnath landscape. The stupa's cylindrical base, adorned with intricate carvings and inscriptions, rises to a height of 43.6 meters (143 feet). The stupa's dome, a symbol of the Buddha's enlightenment, is crowned by a chhatra, or parasol, that signifies his spiritual authority.

The Chaukhandi Stupa, another prominent landmark in Sarnath, is believed to mark the spot where the Buddha met his five former companions after attaining enlightenment. The stupa, originally a terraced temple built in the 5th century CE, was later enhanced by an octagonal tower added by Emperor Akbar in the 16th century. The stupa's unique architecture, a blend of Buddhist and Mughal styles, reflects the diverse cultural influences that have shaped the region over centuries.

The Mulagandhakuti Vihara, a modern temple built in the early 20th century, is a place of great reverence for Buddhists. The temple houses a beautiful statue of the Buddha in a preaching posture, his right hand raised in the Abhaya mudra, the gesture of fearlessness. The temple's walls are adorned with exquisite murals depicting scenes from the Buddha's life and his teachings.

The Sarnath Archaeological Museum, located near the Dhamek Stupa, is a treasure trove of Buddhist art and artifacts. The museum's collection includes sculptures, inscriptions, and relics that date back to the Mauryan and Gupta periods. The museum's most prized possession is the Ashoka Lion Capital, a magnificent sculpture of four Asiatic lions standing back to back, which was adopted as the national emblem of India.

The Ashoka Pillar, another important monument in Sarnath, is a monolithic column erected by Emperor Ashoka in the 3rd century BCE. The pillar, made of polished sandstone, stands 15.2 meters (50 feet) tall and is inscribed with the Edicts of Ashoka, a set of fourteen inscriptions that outline the emperor's policy of dharma, or righteousness.

Sarnath is not just a collection of ancient monuments; it is a living testament to the enduring legacy of the Buddha. The city is home to several monasteries and meditation centers where monks and nuns from various Buddhist traditions reside and practice. These monastic communities play a vital role in preserving and propagating the Buddha's teachings, offering guidance and support to seekers on their spiritual journey.

The Mahabodhi Society Temple, a modern temple complex, is a hub of Buddhist activity in Sarnath. The temple houses a Bodhi tree, a descendant of the original tree under which the Buddha attained enlightenment, and a statue of the Buddha in a meditative posture. The temple complex also has a library, a museum, and a meditation center, providing a space for spiritual learning and practice.

The Sarnath International Nyingma Institute, established by the Dalai Lama in 1969, is a center for the study and practice of Tibetan Buddhism. The institute offers courses in Buddhist philosophy, meditation, and Tibetan language, attracting students from all over the world.

The Thai Temple, a beautiful temple built in traditional Thai style, is another popular pilgrimage site in Sarnath. The temple's serene atmosphere and intricate decorations make it a peaceful haven for meditation and reflection.

Sarnath's spiritual landscape is not limited to temples and

monasteries. The city's deer park, a sprawling expanse of greenery, is a reminder of the Buddha's first sermon, where he preached to a gathering of five ascetics. The deer park, with its tranquil ambiance and abundance of wildlife, is a popular spot for meditation and contemplation.

Sarnath, with its rich history, sacred sites, and vibrant spiritual community, is a place that awakens the soul and nourishes the spirit. It is a place where one can connect with the essence of Buddhism, delve deeper into its teachings, and embark on a transformative journey towards self-discovery and enlightenment.

ϷϷϷ

TWENTY-SIX
SUMMARY

India, a land steeped in spirituality and diverse cultural heritage, offers a multitude of pilgrimage sites that beckon devotees and seekers from all walks of life. These sacred destinations, each with its unique charm and significance, provide a transformative experience, allowing individuals to connect with the divine and embark on a journey of self-discovery. From the ancient city of Varanasi, where the Ganges whispers eternal truths, to the Himalayan abode of Lord Shiva in Kedarnath, each pilgrimage site offers a glimpse into the rich tapestry of India's spiritual traditions.

Varanasi, the spiritual heart of India, is a city that resonates with the rhythmic chants of prayers and the fragrance of incense. The Ganges River, a lifeline for millions and a sacred entity revered as a goddess, flows through the heart of the city, its ghats buzzing with activity as devotees perform rituals, priests offer prayers, and pilgrims take a holy dip in its sacred waters. The city's labyrinthine alleyways lead to ancient temples, such as the Kashi Vishwanath Temple dedicated to Lord Shiva, where the golden spire shimmers in the sunlight, beckoning devotees from far and wide.

Rishikesh, nestled amidst the foothills of the Himalayas, is a sanctuary of yoga and spirituality. It is here, in the tranquil ambiance of ashrams and yoga schools, that seekers from all corners of the globe come to delve into the profound wisdom of yoga, meditation, and philosophy. The Ganges River, a source of life and spiritual renewal, flows through Rishikesh, its ghats abuzz with activity as devotees perform rituals and seek blessings.

Haridwar, the "Gateway to God," is a spiritual portal for millions of pilgrims who come to immerse themselves in the purifying waters of the Ganges and embark on a transformative journey. Har Ki Pauri, the most sacred ghat in Haridwar, is the epicenter of spiritual activity, where the evening aarti, a ritual offering of light and prayers, creates a mesmerizing spectacle.

Amritsar, home to the Golden Temple, is synonymous with Sikh devotion and a symbol of unity and equality. The Golden Temple, a beacon of spiritual radiance, draws millions of devotees who come to seek the blessings of the Guru Granth Sahib, the Sikh holy scripture, and partake in the langar, the community kitchen that embodies the Sikh principle of selfless service.

Bodh Gaya, where Gautama Buddha attained enlightenment, is a pilgrimage site of immense spiritual importance for Buddhists. The Mahabodhi Temple, a magnificent structure that stands as a testament to the enduring legacy of the Buddha, draws millions of devotees who come to pay homage to the enlightened one and retrace his footsteps towards liberation.

Dharamshala, the abode of the Dalai Lama, is a sanctuary of Tibetan Buddhism in exile. The Tsuglagkhang Complex, the Dalai Lama's official residence and the spiritual heart of Dharamshala, is a place of immense significance for Tibetans and Buddhists alike. The complex houses the Namgyal Monastery, the Tibet Museum, and the Library of Tibetan Works and Archives, preserving the rich cultural and spiritual heritage of Tibet.

Tirupati, home to the Tirumala Venkateswara Temple, is one of the most revered and visited pilgrimage sites in the world. The temple, dedicated to Lord Venkateswara, a manifestation of Lord Vishnu, attracts millions of devotees who come to seek the blessings of the deity and experience the divine aura that permeates the sacred hilltop shrine.

Rameshwaram, an island off the southeastern coast of India, is home to the Ramanathaswamy Temple, a magnificent shrine dedicated to Lord Shiva. The temple, with its towering gopurams, sprawling corridors, and intricately carved pillars, is an architectural marvel that draws pilgrims who come to seek the blessings of Lord Shiva and experience the divine aura that permeates this sacred island.

Madurai, an ancient city in Tamil Nadu, is synonymous with the Meenakshi Amman Temple, a sprawling complex that stands as a testament to the rich cultural and architectural heritage of the region. The temple, dedicated to Goddess Meenakshi and her consort Sundareswarar, is a living monument that encapsulates the essence of Dravidian art, architecture, and spirituality.

Kanchipuram, known as the "City of a Thousand Temples," boasts a rich tapestry of architectural marvels, each a testament to the devotion and craftsmanship of generations past. The Kailasanathar Temple, a UNESCO World Heritage Site, and the Ekambareswarar Temple, with its thousand-pillared hall, are just two examples of the city's rich temple heritage.

Ujjain, an ancient city steeped in mythology and spirituality, is home to the Mahakaleshwar Jyotirlinga, a revered shrine dedicated to Lord Shiva. The temple, with its majestic architecture and serene ambiance, draws millions of pilgrims who come to seek the blessings of Lord Shiva and experience the transformative power of his presence.

Pushkar, a city nestled in the heart of Rajasthan, is home to the Brahma Temple, one of the few temples in the world dedicated to Lord Brahma, the Hindu god of creation. The city is also known for its sacred Pushkar Lake, believed to have been created by Lord Brahma himself.

Shirdi, a small town in Maharashtra, is the home of Sai Baba, a revered saint who transcended religious boundaries and embraced people from all faiths. Sai Baba's teachings of love, compassion, and selfless service continue to inspire millions of devotees who flock to Shirdi to seek his blessings and guidance.

Sabarimala, nestled in the dense forests of the Western Ghats in Kerala, is a pilgrimage site of immense spiritual significance dedicated to Lord Ayyappa. The challenging trek to the shrine is a test of devotion and endurance, and a testament to the unwavering faith of the pilgrims who embark on this spiritual quest.

Kedarnath, nestled amidst the majestic peaks of the Garhwal Himalayas, is a place of profound spiritual significance and home to the Kedarnath Temple, a shrine dedicated to Lord Shiva. The challenging trek to the shrine is an arduous yet spiritually rewarding experience that attracts devotees from all walks of life.

Badrinath, another revered shrine nestled in the Himalayas, is dedicated to Lord Vishnu. The Badrinath Yatra, the pilgrimage to Badrinath, is a journey of faith, devotion, and self-discovery, involving a challenging trek through rugged terrain and offering a transformative experience for the devotees.

Hemkund Sahib, a revered Sikh pilgrimage site nestled amidst the breathtaking Himalayas, is a testament to the unwavering devotion and spiritual fortitude of the Sikh community. Situated at a high altitude, Hemkund Sahib is one of the highest altitude Gurudwaras in the world, offering a unique spiritual experience for all who embark on the arduous journey to this sacred site.

These are just a few of the many pilgrimage sites that India has to offer. Each site, with its unique history, cultural significance, and spiritual ambiance, provides a unique and transformative experience for the seeker. Whether it is seeking blessings at the temples, participating in the vibrant festivals, or simply immersing oneself in the serene atmosphere, these pilgrimage sites offer a glimpse into the rich tapestry of India's spiritual traditions.

Citation And References

This book represents the culmination of extensive research and meticulous analysis, incorporating a diverse range of sources, including numerous books, scholarly studies, and personal experiences. Additionally, I have scoured various websites to gather relevant information and data essential for the compilation of this work. I have taken every precaution to ensure the accuracy of the information presented and have diligently cited all sources to acknowledge their contributions.

Despite these efforts, the possibility of inadvertent errors remains. I deeply value the insights of my readers and appreciate any feedback that can help identify and rectify such inaccuracies. I encourage you to bring any discrepancies to my attention.

Your feedback is not only welcome but crucial, as it will aid in correcting current editions and enhancing the content of future ones. I am committed to maintaining the highest standards of accuracy and reliability in my work and thank you for your support and understanding.

Additionally, I firmly uphold the principle of freedom of speech and expression as guaranteed under Article 19(1)(a) of the Constitution of India, and I respect the diverse viewpoints and expressions of all readers.

ppp

Other Books Of The Author

1. Empowering Minds: A Journey into Women's Self-Discovery and Power
2. The Dynamics of Motivation: Catalyzing Thought into Action
3. Meditation and Mental Well Being: The Path to Inner Peace and Clarity
4. The Psychology of Child Education: Nurturing Future Generations
5. Ethical Enlightenment: A Modern Guide to Living with Integrity
6. Voices of Empowerment: Stories of Women Rising Against Odds
7. Social Psychology in Everyday Life: Understanding Human Connections
8. The Essence of Motivational Speaking: Inspiring Change in Others
9. Balancing Acts: Women, Work, and the Will to Lead
10. Guiding with Grace: Raising Children with Compassion and Awareness
11. The Power of Positive Aging: Embracing Life After Fifty
12. Building Resilient Communities: Social Work in Action
13. The Ethical Educator: Principles for Teaching and Learning
14. From Insight to Impact: Social Psychology for a Better World
15. The Ethics of Empathy: A Guide to Ethical Living
16. The Science of Empowering the Self: Navigating Life's Challenges with Psychological Wisdom
17. The Mindful Conscious Leader: Meditation Techniques for Modern Management
18. Pioneering Spirit: Women's Pathways to Leadership and Empowerment
19. Feeling to Healing: The Role of Emotional Intelligence in Child Development
20. Transformative Talks and Words of Inspiration: Insights into Motivational Oratory

Bhajan

101. Pilgrimage of the Soul: Spiritual Journeys in India

ᗑᗑᗑ

Contact

Dr. Minakshi Bansal
Social Activist
Ahmedabad, Gujarat, Bharat
minakshiindiag20@yahoo.com

ᐅᐅᐅ

|| LOKAHA SAMASTHAHA SUKHINO BHAVANTU ||

www.ingramcontent.com/pod-product-compliance
Lightning Source LLC
Chambersburg PA
CBHW031553150726
47990CB00001B/337